Phonics, Too!

How to teach skills in a balanced
language program

Jan Wells
Linda Hart-Hewins

Pembroke Publishers Limited

© 1994 Pembroke Publishers
538 Hood Road
Markham, Ontario L3R 3K9

Canadian Cataloguing in Publication Data

Wells, Jan, 1948-
  Phonics, too! : how to teach skills in a
balanced language program

Includes bibliographical references and index.
ISBN 1-55138-024-2

1. Reading (Elementary) – Phonetic method.
2. Language arts (Primary). I. Hart-Hewins, Linda.
II. Title.

LB1525.3.W45 1994   372.4'145   C94-930141-8

Editor: Joanne Close
Design: John Zehethofer
Typesetting: Jay Tee Graphics Ltd.

This book was produced with the generous assistance of the government of Ontario through the Ministry of Culture and Communications.

Printed and bound in Canada by Webcom
9 8 7 6 5 4 3

Contents

Introduction

Fifteen-month-old Callum is reading a book with his grandmother. She turns the pages of Jan Pienkowski's *Zoo*, a tiny board book just big enough for the baby's fist to grasp. As they look at each picture Callum's grandmother names the animals: bear, dog, gorilla. Callum responds by making **bbb** sounds when he sees the bear. He looks down at his dog when he sees the picture of the dog. When he looks at the picture of the gorilla he turns the book over to show his grandmother that the same picture is to be found on the front cover. Callum does not yet have many words in his vocabulary, but he is already a reader. He knows that objects — people, places, things — can be represented in pictures. Callum also knows that pictures have meaning. They correspond to things in his world. When he picks up a book that is upside down, he automatically turns it the right way round. As his life experiences accumulate and his world view widens so will his awareness of the way in which we use symbols to represent our experience.

Callum is learning to be a user a words — a maker of meaning. The roots of literacy are being established through the interactions that occur in his life around stories, books, and rhymes, and through the naming of objects and the simultaneous matching of the sound of words to their shape in print. There are many things that he must learn about language before he will be able to read words fluently, but the process of learning has begun. Whatever the first language the baby learns, the roots of future reading and writing skills lie in the learning of language as a symbolic system, a means of representing ideas and communicating them to others.

Learning to read independently will not be the end of the process for there is much to be learned about literacy. Literacy in different contexts with different styles and forms of print for different purposes are some of the more refined meanings that will be learned later. For children whose first language is other than English there will be the learning of reading and writing skills in the language of the school, as well as the language of the home.

What are the skills that Callum and other children must acquire? What is the knowledge that must be in place for him to become a life-long reader? What attitude or disposition toward reading and writing is necessary for him to become literate? Can we identify these skills separately, even though we know they are learned together and not in isolation? We think it is important to *identify* the parts in order to understand the whole. We, as teachers, want to be responsive to the needs of the children: if we can identify the components of literacy development then we can watch children and observe the moment when abilities become established. We will know what to look for when making a plan for children's learning needs; we will see what children can do and be ready to nudge them toward the next achievement. Our responses will be more effective in providing the child with linguistic data. We will be able to assess the success of our teaching, and make decisions about the sorts of activities that we are providing in our classrooms. We will be able to create the conditions that will help to make children life-long readers and writers. But what do we mean by literacy? What are our goals?

For many, learning to read and write was dominated by instruction in phonics, spelling, punctuation, and grammar. In such a skills-driven curriculum, individual aspects of learning to read and write (phonics and grammar) were isolated and emphasized almost to the exclusion of other important aspects of literacy. They were not viewed as parts in the service of a larger whole — they were the whole. Literacy was equated with the ability to say the words that were printed on the page. Accuracy in reproducing the words of others was more important than understanding what those words meant, more important, too, than putting ideas into words. Understanding and searching for meaning was postponed until some later date when the mechanics of language use had been mastered. Unfortunately, for many learners, these skills were like beautiful tires on a vehicle that didn't have an engine. It looked good but it didn't move. As a result there are many adults today who know how to read but who never do so for pleasure. Literacy is much more than the ability to bark out words or produce perfect spelling scores on Friday tests. The ideas in this book are founded on the following definition: *Literacy involves bringing meaning to text*.

Reading is first and foremost a meaning-driven enterprise. In the act of reading, the reader must think about what the words mean, both individually and as a whole. Readers are active participants in constructing the meaning of the text as they bring their prior knowledge to bear upon the words to fit them to their existing world view, or schema. A single word triggers a host of associations in the mind while words in combination interact with one another and with the reader's schema to create new meanings. Both reading and writing are acts of constructing meaning and our comprehension of what we read depends upon our prior knowledge. With no such knowledge of a topic, we are in trouble as readers; our level of understanding decreases in proportion to our experience. There are texts that challenge all of us in some way; areas in which we can all be said to be illiterate because our prior knowledge of the subject is sparse or non-existent. A tractor mechanic can understand a repair manual that is incomprehensible to those of us who do not have experience of tractors. Literacy, in this sense, is dependent upon context. Who wrote the text and for what purpose? What prior knowledge do you need in order to be able to understand it? Can you access prior knowledge to make sense of the text?

Literacy Is Social

The social context in which writing is produced determines the nature of the text. Text has definite purposes and functions; a newspaper article on baseball differs from a story in a children's book and an advertisement in the phone directory. Each has its appropriate style and typical form. The way in which each of these texts is read is also dependent upon the context, the setting, and the purposes of the reader. Choosing a children's book in the library we skim it quickly. When we read it out loud to the class we give it expression and try to bring the book to life. There is no single way to read and write. The literate person is able to adjust the nature of his or her reading and writing to fit social contexts. Reading a memo at work is different from reading a textbook to find information for an essay. A poem about logging and its effect on the environment is different in form and style from the same information written as a scientific report.

Literacy is part of everyday life and takes place in different social settings. The nature of the literacy act is somewhat dependent upon that setting. Is it a private or a public act? Do others depend upon my interpretation and reaction? What will happen as a result of this reading or writing? Answers to such questions determine the nature of the literacy event.

Literacy Involves Interpreting the Meaning

Have you noticed how a book comes to life for you if you have been to the places mentioned in the story? Visual images accompany the words; sounds and smells may be evoked that go beyond the words on the page. Words are produced by people for people, to inform them, entertain them, excite them, move them. Behind every text there is a writer with a purpose and meaning intentions that she or he hopes to communicate to the reader. Every reader, however, brings a personal agenda to the reading. Meanings can only be a joint construction — a transaction between text and reader. We have already said that comprehension depends upon prior knowledge, but this is not a one-way process in which the reader somehow uses his or her experience to uncover the writer's intentions. Rather, it is a two-way process — an interaction between the words and the meanings we bring to them. Our background knowledge influences the way in which we interpret or respond to texts. Do we find a story sad or merely silly? Do we agree with the writer's opinions? Answers to these questions are personal and dependent upon who we are as people.

The meaning of any text, then, is not fixed but rather a transaction between reader and writer, between the words and the meaning we bring to them. In this sense each reading is unique as each reader is unique. We can never know precisely the sense that each of us makes of a particular text.

Comprehension is linked closely to our cultural and social experience, which in multicultural classrooms is a significant factor. The meanings of words, the significance of events, relationships between people, what is acceptable behavior, and how people talk to each other are culturally specific or influenced. Though we find common ground in deciding broadly what a story or poem is about, each person interprets the text slightly differently. This accounts for the widely different tastes of readers. Books speak to us in different ways at different times. Reading is a much more untidy business than we thought.

So how do we reach common understandings? How can we have consensus or agree to differ? Being literate involves being a member of a literate community, sharing ways of thinking and being with others who are literate but having our own unique responses to each text we read. A significant part of our definition of literacy, then, is that it must involve *talk* about texts. Finding meanings in literature or in other kinds of writing is made possible when readers talk to each other about their interpretations, questions, and ideas. Belonging to a literate community involves the ability to share ideas about writing and what it means, and implies a willingness to engage in discussion about writing with others who have read the same thing. Literacy is holistic because it involves reading, writing, speaking, and listening.

Literacy Involves Understanding the Surface Features of Print

How does the symbol system work to represent language on the printed page? Reading involves the ability to recognize and interpret words as they appear on the page and the ability to pronounce them. Writing involves knowing how to apply the rules of grammar and how to spell accurately. These skills are necessary. To return to the car analogy; a vehicle with an engine missing can't move, however beautiful its tires. Skills are like wheels; they have purposes within the context of shaping and honing a piece of writing or in making meaning from a written text.

The skills of encoding ideas in written form are the tools of the writer's trade: vocabulary, spelling, punctuation, and grammar are all necessary parts of the whole enterprise of being a writer. True communication takes place when a writer can manipulate the language with deliberate expertise. Accuracy is important and in some contexts essential. Knowing the conventions of writing and how to use them effectively is part of being a successful user of language.

Readers also need many skills if they are to understand and interpret the written text before them. Some of the specific skills that successful readers develop include automatic recognition of many words and their phonetic elements; reading for specific purposes; knowing how to change their reading style to meet needs such as finding information by skimming and scanning a text; reading a manual by focusing on headings; and developing an open, interpretive, or "aesthetic" stance toward poetry.

Using phonics in reading is one area of skill development. Phonics on their own, however, do not constitute the act of reading and are useless in isolation. While developing readers need to be introduced to phonics they must see their use in the service of a larger goal — getting meaning from print. Recognizing and using the alphabetic system is *part* of the whole enterprise.

Literacy for us, then, is a constructive, creative act involving the interaction of ideas and not simply the ability to say the words printed on a page. It involves being able to create meanings, as well as being able to receive, interpret, appreciate, and critique the meanings of others. It is reading, writing, talking, listening, and viewing. Being literate is empowering in both a personal and a social sense, and is far reaching in its implications for learning and thinking.

Our model incorporates the learning of skills into the search for meaning; all parts of the model are viewed as components to help the learner make meaning from the texts they are reading or creating. This view of literacy has implications for the use of the term "skills." We believe that learners need all of the following skills if they are to be independent life-long readers and writers. When we use the term skills we refer to the ability to:

- seek and use prior knowledge in the search for meaning in text;
- seek alternate and competing interpretations of text;
- recognize text as context dependent;
- read in ways appropriate to the context and purpose;
- use writing to generate and explore meaning;
- use talk and writing as ways of exploring and exchanging ideas about the meaning of text; and
- manipulate the technical aspects of the language that allow meanings to be encoded and decoded.

As teachers change their practices in response to increased understanding of how language is learned and is used to learn, questions arise around the issue of how best to teach the skills that learners will require. This book is a response to the need that many teachers have expressed to explore the possibilities for teaching skills within the framework of the whole language classroom. Contrary to popular belief, whole language teachers do teach skills. They just do it better than before!

In this book we set out to answer the following questions:

- How is literacy best learned?
- What are the range of skills that fluent and successful readers and writers of English employ?
- How are these skills learned?
- Is there a particular order in which they should be learned and, if so, what is it?
- How can teachers best help children to learn the skills necessary for success and appropriate to their stage of development?

We have organized the ideas in the book according to three broad stages of development, Beginning, Developing, and Fluent Readers and Writers. For each stage we describe the children; what they look like, what they can do, what they feel about reading and writing, and what they need to learn. Suggested teaching ideas for meeting the needs of learners are organized under three headings:

- Demonstrations: things that teachers can do with the whole class, with small groups, and with individual children to demonstrate uses of language.
- Responses: ideas for organizing conferences and for responding to children's work.
- Classroom Activities: ideas for activities using language that children can do independently, alone, or with friends that give practice and build confidence in the use of language.

CHAPTER ONE

An Overview

How Is Literacy Learned?

When we buy a "reading program," we are selecting a product that has been designed by people with a set of beliefs about how reading is learned that has been carefully worked out. What thinking underlies the methodology? What theories of learning are at work here? We need to think about methodology and materials, not in terms of right or wrong, the latest trend, or because someone else tells us to do it, but in light of personal beliefs and values. The starting point for this is in identifying and articulating our own philosophy.

There is not "one right way" to teach. Learning is a complex, individual process. We want to make learning easy for all children, and to know more about how they learn and how we can best help them. We must be open to new learning as we work with children and our peers. While we can be sure of our beliefs, we can always be open to new ways of interpreting them.

Thinking about our practice is an ever-changing process. In writing this book we have become aware of ways in which our thinking has developed since we wrote *Real Books for Reading*. We think it is important to try out ideas, watch children carefully, respond to their developing needs, and adapt ideas to best suit the children. This involves constant adjustment and responsiveness. It is a creative process that demands imagination and dedication, as well as organizational skill and enormous amounts of energy. When we teach reflectively we are constantly rewarded, often surprised and delighted, but never bored.

The ideas in this book are organized around three phases of

development. We know that there are children at each of these phases in most primary classrooms. We know, too, that in more senior classes there are children who are not yet successful independent readers. Some of the strategies will be useful to teachers working with these children and to teachers working with children for whom English is a second language.

Our ability to teach successfully depends upon our understanding of the full growth continuum and our ability to recognize where a child's needs fall on that continuum. This allows us to choose appropriate strategies for individual and groups of children while enabling us to plan programs that reflect the diversity of learners. Our underlying philosophy is that our classrooms must be places where children can learn and grow in ways that respect who they are, where they come from, and what they bring with them. We must plan curriculum that meets their needs as learners. This means that rather than providing one learning experience with one set of materials and one way for the children to communicate their learning, we must provide a variety of experiences, responses, and materials.

This does not mean a lowering of standards or an acceptance of a "free to be" philosophy. On the contrary, it promotes high achievement and is founded on the principle that high teacher expectations promote high student achievement. Membership of the community of learners comes with its responsibilities; school is a place in which learning happens. It is the teacher's job to establish this principle.

Our goals are to educate children to the best of their individual potential and to hope that they will grow up to find that reading and writing are a meaningful, essential part of their adult lives. We want our children to be life-long readers; to be members of the literate community; to share ideas, experiences, and feelings through the printed word.

So how do we believe literacy is learned?

Literacy Is Learned Developmentally

Learners pass through stages of competency. A five year old who is able to write her name and tell stories from pictures is at one level of literacy. There are things that child can do, and things she needs to learn. In any class there will be learners at different stages in their growth. Children bring a range of experiences, knowledge, skills, and attitudes toward learning. We believe that teachers need to be not only sensitive to individual differences, but to see it as an important principle in organizing the language program. In selecting classroom activities and materials, we must take the diversity of learners into account.

We also believe that literacy is learned through interaction with others engaged in literacy. It is the most natural thing in the world for children to want to be able to understand the words they see around them and use those written words in the same way that they learned to talk.

That doesn't mean that literacy "just happens" and all we have to do is wait for it and watch it emerge! The important thing that parents and teachers do is provide the conditions that enable this type of learning to take place. Brian Cambourne, the Australian educator and researcher, has given us a model of the conditions necessary for the acquisition of literacy. Cambourne describes conditions that need to be in place before children can learn to read and write. The following headings are from his work, the descriptions are our interpretation.

Immersion

Children learn to talk because they are surrounded daily by it. Caregivers talk to babies and not only expect them to understand, they actually impute meaning into the babies' utterances long before these sound like words. Babies are immersed in spoken language from which data they construct working hypotheses about how language works and what it means. Learning about written language happens in the same way. When children are immersed in language activities, in an environment which is full of print, then conditions are created in which they can begin to construct ideas about the mechanics and purpose of writing. They need to see it, hear it, and most importantly, use it to test developing hypotheses.

The teacher's role is to create a language-rich environment in which the children are immersed in reading and writing activities every day.

Demonstration

Demonstrations, which can take many forms, are direct illustrations of how something is done or how something works. For example, when a parent reads a story to a child there is a demonstration of how the symbols on the page become spoken words. When a teacher writes a poem on a chart, there is a demonstration of how spoken words become print. All learning requires demonstrations. We must see what we are to learn before we can learn it.

The teacher's role is to provide purposeful, appropriate demonstrations of language in use.

Expectation

Most children come to school with expectations that they will learn to read and write. They know that it is important and they want to be able to do it. This expectation of success is an important component in the enterprise of learning to read and write. Teachers must show that they share this expectation through their responses and actions. They must communicate confidence in each learner's ability to succeed.

The teacher's responsibility is to have high expectations of the success of all learners, and to foster an environment where children are encouraged, supported, praised, and their successes celebrated.

Approximation

As children learn language they produce immature forms to express meaningful ideas. A baby wanting a drink will cry "ginga!" and his caregiver will respond by saying, "You want a drink of water, do you?" If the child had to wait to learn to say, "Please can I have a drink of water?" before he got his drink, he might not survive! Language is used meaningfully and we respond to it as if it had been used accurately. Since we attend more to meaning and less to form when we interact with children, we provide them with the opportunity to test their hypotheses about language. The reply they receive gives them more data upon which to draw. Next time the child wants a drink he might try "wa wa" or perhaps "want ginga" in an approximation of the form he is seeking. This principle must also be applied to the learning of reading and writing, which are foremost acts of meaning making. We must respond to the meanings that children are making. What do they intend to write? What sense do

18

they make of text? Their initial efforts will not be technically accurate, but they represent their current state of knowledge. Accurate word recognition and spelling are not the *first* goals of an early literacy program. These come later when the child has sufficient mastery of the written language and the confidence to be able to deal with these features. Working hypotheses must be tested and refined until the learner is satisfied that they are accurate. The children's efforts can be viewed as windows into their minds that show us what they know and what they need to learn. Our instruction must be tailored to fit the needs revealed in current approximations.

The teacher's role is to recognize approximations as evidence of learning and achievement; to monitor the learning over time; and to use approximations to determine what the child needs to do next.

Use

Children need time and opportunity to use their developing language skills every day, both alone and with others. The classroom must be a place where children get to do things with language. They need to be reading and writing more than they need to be listening to the teacher tell them how to read and write! The most important thing a child can do in learning to read is to read and write.

The teacher's role is to organize language activities that allow children to read and write every day.

Response

This refers to the feedback that the learner receives. "You want a drink of water do you?" is feedback in response to "ginga," and provides linguistic data. The responses we make to children's talk, writing, and attempts to read are a crucial part of our teaching. Through our responses we can encourage the learner's engagement with learning; provide demonstrations of mature models that offer data for the learner's developing hypotheses; give specific responses contingent upon the learner's particular needs; and give the learner license to take risks that will lead to further learning.

The teacher's role is to respond in supportive, informative, and encourag-

ing ways to children's efforts. The teacher organizes opportunities for response systematically through reading and writing conferences.

Responsibility

There is no perfect program that if offered in the right order, at the right time, and in perfect lessons will make children learn. It is the learner who has responsibility for learning how to use language and who will decide which aspect of any language act has significance. When we provide demonstrations of language use, we have no way of knowing or legislating to which part of the demonstration a child will attend. Fragmenting, or decontextualizing language instruction, is counterproductive and confusing. Grammar and phonics skills must be learned in the context of meaningful language activities.

The teacher's responsibility is to offer a range of opportunities for the children to engage in authentic acts of language use that embrace their individual interests, strengths, and differences.

These are the conditions that must be present for literacy to develop. When they exist, learners become engaged with learning, seeing it as important and relevant to their needs. School is seen as a place where interesting things happen.

The underlying principles that guide our practices can be summarized as follows:

- Language is learned by doing meaningful things with language; it is meaning driven. Skills are learned in use, not in isolation.
- Literacy is learned developmentally and naturally, when the conditions for learning are provided.
- Children are individuals, diverse in background experiences, learning styles, and personalities. They learn best when their individual needs are recognized and provided for.
- Children need to see the purpose for learning and to find it meaningful in their lives. It must be "to do with them."

We will look first at the child at each of the three phases of development. We will then explore methods of demonstration and responding to children. Finally we will outline games and activities that help to make learning to read and write enjoyable.

CHAPTER TWO

A Description of the Children

The Beginning Reader and Writer

Typically children at this stage are referred to as pre-readers. They may even be assessed in terms of their "reading readiness." Many children enter kindergarten at this stage with some, but not all, of the attributes of a successful reader in place. Most are not yet able to decode words that they have not seen before. They may recognize some words and know whole books by heart, but if asked if they could read would say, "Not yet but I'm learning." As writers they know that marks on a page represent spoken words, but their writing, while meaningful to them, cannot be read by others. Acknowledging that they have much knowledge of literacy and are not without awareness of reading and writing, we will refer to them as Beginning Readers and Writers.

I recently observed a group of pre-schoolers during story hour at the local library. These children had a high expectation of this event! The excitement level was up as the librarian took her seat and produced the first book from the bag. She held up the cover and asked, "Does anyone know this one?" "Pig Pig" called out some of the children, recognizing the character on the cover. "I know that. I know how to read. I'm five," said one young person confidently. The children listened as the reading began but there was almost constant interruption as they called out questions and comments. "Who's Pig Pig?" "What's he doing?" "They're having breakfast." "Where's the cat?" "There's the cat." The children engaged with the book, with the pictures, and with one another as the librarian read, paused, answered questions, and asked some of her own. ''Where's he going in his rocket?'' she asked. The group responded, ''The moon!''

These children expected to be entertained and amused by the book. They know that books are of interest; that stories will be fun. They have positive attitudes toward books and stories at this stage, partly because their experiences are almost always pleasurable. First, there is the closeness of an experience shared with others, on a warm lap or in a group of friends. And then there are the stories; humorous, exciting, magical, confirming, frightening, or comforting, but always powerful. Stories occupy a special place in the imaginative life of young children who often have favorites that they demand to hear over and over again. Most parents have had the experience of reading a treasured story so many times that the words becomes automatic. Woe betide the bored reader who tries to take a shortcut by abbreviating the story or changing the words!

The pleasure that young children find in books is often transferred to their play and they will choose to look at books when they are alone or with friends. They will role play themselves as readers, holding the book the way the teacher does and reciting the words they make up in a sing-song voice.

At this stage in their reading development, children look at pictures and expect that the words they hear will refer to those pictures. In other words, they expect that the language of books will be logical in the same way that the print on packaging is logical. When you see a can of Coke you know that Coke will be inside, not tuna. Similarly, when the picture shows a pig in a rocket ship, you can expect that the story will be about a pig in a rocket ship. Pictures are part of early reading as children make predictions from them about the possible meaning of the print. Many of the older primers denied children this information: pictures were sometimes accompanied by words that didn't correspond. I remember listening to child after child read ''Jane and Peter are looking at the butterfly.'' The text read, ''Here is Peter. Here is Jane.'' The children were ''reading the picture.'' To make these predictions, children draw upon their prior knowledge deliberately and with purpose because they know that reading is making meaning. One of the pre-schoolers in the library did this when he called out, ''He's going to fall off and scrape his knee'' when he saw the picture of Pig Pig riding his bike and heard the words, ''Please be careful.'' Although it sounds like guessing, it is reading, using predictions to make meaning from print.

At this early stage of literacy development, children learn that print carries information. They live in an environment in which print is all around them — on signs, packaging, television commercials, and everywhere in the street. This "environmental print" refers to places and things and tells you something. Children have a natural curiosity about these words and often ask, "What does that say?" If they get answers, they begin to build up a repertoire of words known by sight, learned by frequency of occurrence in familiar contexts. These words are highly context dependent, that is, they may be read and understood in the context in which they occur, but may not be recognized when isolated from that situation.

Early on children learn that spoken words can be represented by writing; they know that squiggles which appear around us tell us things we need to know. In their early attempts at written communication, children will imitate the look of written words by drawing squiggles, lines, and letter-like symbols. They will "read" these to us, imputing meaning to the symbols on the page.

I went swimming with my Dad and he made a big splash!

Children, although they know that these squiggles represent meanings, do not yet know how this works. They may know some letters by name, especially those that make up their name or those of family members. They use these letters repeatedly in their writing.

The names of the letters become familiar through the activity of singing or chanting the alphabet. Children naturally learn the twenty-six letter names before they learn the sounds that these symbols may represent (with the exception of a few familiar words — names, signs, etc.).

They have not, however, learned the alphabetic principle — each letter of the alphabet in English represents one or more sounds, or phonemes, and that phonemes combine in speech to make words that represent meanings. Phonemes are represented graphically by letters and combinations of letters. These graphemes are organized into words composed of morphemes (the smallest linguistic unit that carries meaning), which are separated by spaces on the page. The continuous unbroken flow of speech is divided in certain ways when we write it down, and the sounds we make when we speak are represented by various combinations of letters. Determining where the boundaries are placed and how those letters combine to make words are two of the skills that will be learned during this early stage of development. This knowledge is called phonemic awareness. Recognizing the letters of the alphabet when you see them and knowing what sounds they represent is one part of being able to read. These skills will be in place before we can say that the child has moved onto the next stage, that of the Developing Reader and Writer.

What is important to think about is how much of this knowledge about sound-symbol correspondence needs to be deliberately taught. This question lies at the heart of the debate about phonics in early reading instruction. It is not a question of whether or not to teach phonics. Rather, it is a question of how, how often, and in what circumstances. Worksheets do NOT teach phonics, they test whether a child knows them or not! If you can fill in the blanks with the missing letters then you are showing that you know those letters. If you cannot do it, then the worksheet won't help you to learn. The sounds the letters make must be learned through real reading and writing experiences and through rhymes. Phonemic awareness is fostered through traditional nursery rhymes and word games. Children who have a rich knowledge of rhymes develop the ability to pay attention to sounds within words more easily.

Listed here are the characteristics of the Beginning Reader and Writer. These are the skills, the knowledge, and the attitudes that we can observe in a child at this stage. Think of a young child that you know. Some, but not all, of these attitudes and behaviors will be present in that child's repertoire. Others, like being able to read pattern books from memory, come into place at the end of this stage of development. What still needs to be learned? The list can help you to do an assessment of the needs of the children in your class. As well it can help you to see which areas you need to be focusing on in your interactions with the children and can highlight things that you need to demonstrate and model in your classroom.

Characteristics of the Beginning Reader and Writer

Name: _____ **Date:** _____

Knowledge of Literacy

The child understands:

	YES	NO	SOME-TIMES
that reading is meaning making — expects print to make sense;			
• that writing is talk written down;			
• that print holds meaning and conveys information;			
• that reading is a worthwhile skill to achieve;			
• that books are enjoyable;			
• that books will be about something related to the pictures.			

Reading Behavior

The child:

	YES	NO	SOME-TIMES
• likes to listen to stories, rhymes, poems;			
• has favorite stories, can't miss a word of old favorites;			
• "role plays" self as a reader, likes to look at books, handles books voluntarily;			
• reads pictures and knows you can predict meaning from them. Draws on prior knowledge to "read";			
• knows how to hold a book and turn the pages one at a time, front to back;			
• understands print directionality. Words in English start on the left and move to the right, and go from top to bottom;			
• can show you words;			
• knows where to find title and author's name;			

	YES	NO	SOME-TIMES
• knows where a story begins and ends;			
• tries to read environmental print, knows some words by sight such as own name and names of family members;			
• reads pattern books, memorizes them holistically;			
• relies heavily on picture clues and on language patterns to aid memorization of text;			
• can hear rhyme;			
• matches beginning and final sounds accurately;			
• does not read word for word;			
• can retell the main events of the story;			
• reads at a literal level;			
• borrows materials to read to others.			

Writing Behavior

These descriptors are shown as a continuum. Children move from random scribbling to representing words with letters.

The child:

	YES	NO	SOME-TIMES
• scribbles and plays with paper and pencil;			
• uses arbitrary symbols to represent sounds or words;			
• uses letters to represent sounds and words but without sound-letter accuracy;			
• writes without spacing;			
• hears only one major sound in a word;			
• hears more than one sound in a word;			
• knows names of letters in sequence;			
• recognizes individual letters and can say their names;			
• has beginnings of accurate sound-letter accuracy, knows some letters by sound and by name.			

The Developing Reader and Writer

These children have experienced the magical moment when words on the page begin to assume individual meanings. They recognize some words, and read simple text and familiar books without help. If it is a first-time reading, they will need support in using the decoding strategies that successful readers use and the teacher has a vital role to play. These children need lots of encouragement to read; they tire easily and can become discouraged if text is too difficult. They have learned a lot about how letters combine to represent the sound of spoken words. Their writing can be read by others although their spelling is still based on the sound of words rather than the patterns and rules of spelling.

As readers they have had considerable experience of books, stories, and print materials, and are familiar with the purposes and functions of writing and reading. They have memorized whole books using rhyme and repetition to help them, and they rely on pictures and their memory to read these familiar books. The breakthrough comes when they begin to see the correspondence of one spoken word to one printed word.

Children at this stage need to continue to read books they know by heart, but they also need to try new books that have a line of print on each page and pictures that give strong clues. We call these books "First Steps." Typically, as they try to read these books aloud, children slow down and read word by word, pointing to each word as they go. If they get stuck they have one main strategy — stop dead and wait for help! This is the stage where strategies for unlocking unknown words must be learned. There are four main things that readers can do:

- look at the pictures — What is happening? What do you see?
- predict from the developing context — What makes sense here?
- predict from the sense of the sentence — What part of speech fits here?
- use clues from the letters in the word and its structure; that is, phonics — What letters can you see? How do they work together to represent sounds? Do you see familiar patterns?

These strategies must be taught and their use encouraged. When a child hesitates and looks for help say, "What can you try?" "What could help you?" What have you tried already?" "What else could you do?" As their experience grows and their confidence increases, children begin to use these strategies independently and integrate them into their repertoire of reading behaviors. While they are learning, however, support them by suggesting ways to unlock a word, providing the opportunity for them to read daily, helping them build stamina, and assisting them as they develop the ability to read silently.

Amongst other strategies, they are learning more about how letters combine to make sounds, using phonics to unlock words by breaking them into syllables and sounding them out. Much of this phonic knowledge is learned in the daily writing program. These children are becoming confident writers who can represent any words that they can say by choosing letters from the alphabet to represent the sounds they hear in the word. Increasingly, they make accurate choices and their writing becomes easier to read. They realize that there are spaces between words and they begin to put these in. Some children begin by marking these spaces with periods or dashes. They begin to include a vowel in every word (although not always the right one), but show evidence that they understand the relationship between vowels and consonants. Each child spells consistently within his or her own writing, using the same groupings of letters when they want to spell a word. Gradually, a bank of words known by sight is built up and high frequency words are spelled correctly. Invented spelling is replaced by traditional spelling as patterns become familiar. The introduction of a personal word book or dictionary to show the child how to edit work is appropriate at this stage.

We like to put four or five new words they are learning at the front of their writing folder. Children know that before sharing their work with us they must first check that these words are spelled accurately. When they have internalized these spellings, they use a highlighter to cross them off.

Intensive reading and writing activity is crucial at this stage. Demonstrations, games, and shared reading experiences are secondary to daily independent reading sessions. Through conferences, the teacher provides the scaffolding that suggests to the child the necessary skills for encoding and decoding print.

The following list describes the knowledge, skills, and attitudes that we typically see in children at this stage.

Characteristics of the Developing Reader and Writer

Name: _____ **Date:** _____

Knowledge of Literacy

The child understands:

	YES	NO	SOME-TIMES
• that reading and writing are meaningful;			
• that they can use reading and writing for their own purposes in many contexts;			
• that they are successful as readers and writers;			
• that readers use strategies to unlock unknown words;			
• that prediction based on meaning is the most important strategy.			

Reading Behavior

The child:

	YES	NO	SOME-TIMES
• reads familiar pattern books and simple picture books fluently;			
• continues to enjoy being read to;			
• begins to widen choice of materials;			
• reads other children's work;			
• uses picture and meaning clues first;			
• develops strategies for unlocking unknown words but needs help;			
• begins to self-correct when meaning is lost, re-reads to find meaning;			
• doesn't give up easily, tackles new material with adult support;			
• reads slowly and haltingly, word by word;			
• reads out loud for the most part but may read silently with familiar print;			

	YES	NO	SOME-TIMES
• begins to use phonic clues:			
knows that letters are important (recognizes that bed and bad are different words);			
knows consonants and consonant digraphs;			
blends consonants together;			
knows long vowel sounds;			
• has developed a bank of words known by sight.			

Writing Behavior

The child:

	YES	NO	SOME-TIMES
• uses writing for different purposes — personal story, non-fiction, poetry;			
• knows stories have a beginning, middle, and end;			
• begins to include dialogue — uses the language of books;			
• uses both consonants and vowels to represent sounds;			
• spells some high-frequency words correctly;			
• begins to use spaces between words;			
• produces writing that can be read by others;			
• represents every syllable in a word;			
• conferences with a friend;			
• is willing to add more to writing;			
• edits a few words independently;			
• begins to use personal dictionary.			

The Fluent Reader and Writer in the Early Years

As children gain confidence they enter the stage of fluent or independent reading. These children are developing independence as readers and writers. They need lots of practice and are developing speed and stamina, consolidating the ability to read silently with comprehension. They are developing skills in the appropriate use of language for diverse purposes, and in the mastery of the conventions of the language that allow them to communicate their purposes effectively.

The skills involved in being more efficient as a reader are often ignored because we tend to think that once children can read they no longer need to be taught how to read. We will discuss ways in which children can become more successful with a range of print materials. We will also consider the skills of successful writing and ways in which we can offer opportunity for these to be developed and established. This includes ideas for teaching spelling, punctuation, and grammar.

Children feel a great sense of accomplishment when they reach this stage. A teacher friend asked her class of seven year olds what achievement made them most proud. "When I learned to read," was the answer given by most. The skills that the children have gained are now refined and consolidated through their independent reading programs. They move into first novels and begin to establish their tastes for authors and genres. This is also the time, however, when some children lose their enthusiasm for reading as books seem too hard to read or too boring. They may level off as readers and lose their confidence. The approach we take to teaching reading at this stage is critical because it may be that through our choice of materials and the activities we impose we inadvertently take away the pleasure of reading and turn it into a chore associated only with school work.

Phonics exercises and worksheets are pointless and frustrating for children. If a child can read then she or he knows all they ever need to know about phonics; the graphophonic cueing system is at their service and they use it when necessary. The children may still need adult support during reading conferences to help them use their phonic knowledge in attacking unknown words. Phonics can help spelling, and in the context of learning how to edit writing it can be helpful for children to be shown how to apply phonics generalizations (see Useful Things to Know About Phonics, p. 48).

Comprehension questions that reduce a text to a series of fill-in-the-blanks are also detrimental to a child's love of reading. The focus of the reading program should be on learning about books and how they can teach, entertain, and amuse us. Once a child can read a whole new world opens up and the horizon is limitless. There are libraries full of children's literature to explore and a host of wonderful children's authors to enjoy. There is no time to waste on activities that are not real reading; children should be reading widely, extensively, and for genuine purposes.

There is still a role for the teacher in demonstrating, modeling, and selecting materials for the classroom and monitoring children's progress. We coach individuals and teach specific reading behaviors to small groups. We have skills in mind that we want the children to develop and we design experiences for them that will help them to become more efficient, flexible, and eclectic readers.

The children are consolidating their ability to express ideas in writing. They use writing for a range of purposes, are becoming faster and more efficient, and are beginning to use writing as a tool for learning in all subjects through brainstorming, listing learning logs, and note making. New skills of editing and revising become the focus of learning to write. The conventional uses of English need to be mastered by children at this stage; patterns of spelling and grammar are learned in the context of the writing program.

Characteristics of the Fluent Reader and Writer in the Early Years

Name: _____   Date: _____

Knowledge of Literacy

The child understands:

	YES	NO	SOME-TIMES
• that reading and writing are meaningful;			
• that they can fulfill purposes through reading and writing, and that reading and writing have many purposes;			
• that they are successful as readers and writers;			
• that writing has different styles and forms depending on the context.			

Reading Behavior

The child:

	YES	NO	SOME-TIMES
• continues to enjoy being read to;			
• enjoys longer, more detailed materials;			
• reads for longer periods. Shows increasing independence when reading;			
• integrates semantic, syntactic, and graphophonic cueing systems to read for meaning from longer, more complex sentence structures;			
• does not need to pay attention to print detail;			
• stops and self-corrects when meaning is lost and does so with ease and confidence;			
• begins to understand how alphabetical order works;			
• uses a dictionary to find the meaning of an unknown word;			
• can use a library, feels comfortable there;			
• responds to literature through talk and writing. Comprehends literally and goes beyond literal comprehension to infer meaning, makes personal connections, describes own feelings.			

Writing Behavior The child:	YES	NO	SOME-TIMES
• writes in different modes: stories, poems, reports, learning logs, etc;			
• reflects reading interests in writing: animals, mystery, family stories, fairy tales;			
• in non-fiction writing: can focus on a topic and give adequate, accurate information;			
shows organization — imitates structures learned through reading non-fiction materials, e.g., table of contents, headings;			
• in narrative writing: can write stories with several episodes;			
begins to establish time, setting, characters;			
uses vocabulary to set mood and atmosphere;			
develops characters with problems to solve and choices to make — they act with consistency;			
with adult support, writes stories with a plausible conclusion;			
• revises own work: begins to substitute, delete, and add information at the level of word, sentence, and episode to improve first drafts;			
begins to use suggestions made by peers and teacher in conferences;			
• edits own work: begins to recognize when familiar words are misspelled;			
uses a personal dictionary or word bank when editing;			
uses a dictionary, understands alphabetization;			
begins to apply spelling rules consistently;			
begins to recognize root words and how they are changed by suffixes and prefixes;			
uses a wide vocabulary and will experiment with word use in first-draft writing;			
recognizes that punctuation is functional and should be used appropriately;			
• refines personal handwriting style — printing is clear and legible.			

Ideas for Demonstrations

The Beginning Reader and Writer

You can do these activities with the whole class or with small groups of children. Remember not to keep young children sitting still for too long and be sure that your demonstrations are appropriate to learning needs. Try not to instruct only in ability groups as mixed ability groups allow you to vary questions and instructions to suit individual learners. The children should never see themselves as part of a fixed group with a particular identity. The following ideas:

- help those children who do not yet understand that reading is meaning making and that writing is talk written down and represented by print;
- develop children's ability to predict meaning from pictures and from the developing context of a story;
- help children establish concepts about print such as directionality, sound-symbol correspondence (phonemic awareness), and the alphabetic principle.

Read Aloud Using a Big Book or a Chart

Make the reading process explicit by describing what you are doing.
1. Before beginning to read the book, talk about the cover; what is this going to be about?
2. Read all the way through for enjoyment and meaning.
3. Talk about what happened; what was the story/poem/chart about?

4. What was the best part? Did the children like it? Discuss their reactions.
5. Read again; on this and subsequent re-readings choose one or two of the following ideas:
   • Ask the children to predict what is going to happen next by looking at the pictures. Always ask, "How do you know?";
   • Talk about details in the pictures; what emotions are characters showing? How do you know?
   • Stop at the end of a line or before a key word such as a character's name or a repeating phrase and let children chime in.
   • Cover the last word of a line or a key word and let children chime in. Ask, "How did you know that it said that?"
   • Show the first letter of a key word and let children chime in.
   • Ask children to find key words in the text and point to them.
   • Show how you turn the pages when you get to the end of the writing.
   • Point to the words as they move from left to right.

Create a Written Message Together

As an example, write a class newsletter that can be sent home once a week outlining activities and events in the classroom. This not only provides a real reason for writing, it also keeps parents in touch with the life of the classroom. Other ideas for shared writing include recipes, recording scientific observations, making lists of the children's ideas during brainstorming, and writing letters.

1. As you write on the chart, ask the children what words you are to write. It is important to decide on the message together — it should be their language that is written, not yours.
2. Talk as you write; show how you represent the spoken words by writing letters.
3. Demonstrate the one-to-one correspondence of spoken word to written word by talking your way through it as you write.
4. Use the language of writing: talk about the letters you use. Talk about the beginning of the word, the end of the word, the middle of the word, sound, space, letter, sentence, spelling, beginning sound, ending sound. Sound out words as you write them.

5. Show how the words are read from left to right across the page.
6. When the message is finished have the children read it together.

Use Environmental Print

There are a number of ways you can use environmental print. Here are some examples that can be done in the classroom and in the school neighborhood.

- Create signs for the classroom together when there is a need, for example "Math Center," "Three people at the sand table," and "Please sweep up when you are finished." Don't label furniture just for the sake of labeling — make useful signs.
- Together with the children, label equipment and the place where it is stored so that they can match the words. As an example, you can line a shelf with construction paper and draw shapes corresponding to the containers for equipment. Scissors go into a tin labeled "Scissors" and the tin sits on a circle also labeled "Scissors."
- Take a walk around the school and read all the signs you can find.
- Go on an "environmental print walk" around the neighborhood. Take a camera and photograph signs. Display these pictures on a bulletin board, or make a book of signs.
- Encourage children to make signs in play situations. Children who wish to leave a block construction undisturbed may make a sign saying "Please do not touch." They can attach labels to their buildings indicating what they are and giving instructions; castle, entrance, please pay here, no parking, etc. In the home corner or dramatic play center there are frequent opportunities for print to be used if materials are provided and their use encouraged. Restaurant menus, telephone messages, hospital waiting lists, and medical prescriptions are examples of the sort of writing that children can do during their play.
- Make a "Book of Bags," using bags from local stores stapled or taped together so they can be read like a book.

A-Z: Ideas for Teaching the Alphabet

While children will learn the names of the alphabet letters before they learn their sounds, chances are they won't learn them in order (letters in their name will be learned first). Knowing the names of the letters of the alphabet is an important predictor of success in reading (Adams, 1990). "Knowing the alphabet," however, involves more than one skill. One must know what the letters look like, what sounds, or phonemes, they represent, and be able to hear those phonemes in words. Discriminating between sounds is the other important predictor of success that Adams found in her exhaustive survey of the research into the teaching of phonics. Knowing the alphabet, then, involves the following skills of visual and auditory discrimination and memory:

- saying the alphabet by rote;
- recognizing an individual letter by name when it is shown. "Can you tell me what this letter is?";
- recognizing an individual letter by sound when it is shown. "Can you tell me which sound this letter makes?";
- correctly identifying a letter by name from an array. "Can you show me which one is the B?";
- correctly identifying a letter to represent a sound in writing. "Which letter do you need to make a **buh** sound?";
- hearing individual sounds in words and discriminating between them. "Which sounds do you hear in this word?"

Demonstrations of what the alphabet looks like and the sounds that the letters make are part of the everyday life of the early primary classroom as we talk about letters and sounds constantly. As well as planned mini-lessons around sounds and letters, those odd moments between other activities or when waiting in line are good opportunities for impromptu games that develop auditory discrimination and alphabetic awareness. At this stage of Beginning Reading the children are learning to hear and use consonants, hearing them in both the initial and final position in words. They also hear and use the long vowel sounds, contrary to the general belief that short vowels must be easier to learn because they are short! As well, children begin to represent words by using the sound that seems most obvious to them. The focus for these children, then, is on learning the sounds of the 21 consonants and the names of the vowels. The consonants are b, c, d, f, g, h, j, k, l, m, n, p, q, r, s, t, v, w, x, y, and z. All but three are regular because they always make the same sound.

C and **g** are exceptions because they can be hard (cat, girl) or soft (ceiling, giant). **Y** is difficult because it says "**ee**" at the end of words (quickly), and combines with vowels in the initial position (yet, young, yacht). These three are usually not used accurately in spelling until later. The rule for soft and hard **g** may be useful as a tool for unlocking unknown words at the next stage of reading.

Several consonants, which combine in words to create only one speech sound, are called the consonant digraphs. They are **ch, th, sh, wh**. At this stage of learning initial and final consonants, it seems sensible to show these letters working together and to introduce children to them in their writing. If they want to spell chair they need a **ch** sound. In playing games that reinforce initial letter sounds we include the consonant digraphs.

Here are some ideas for helping children learn the alphabet. We stress strongly, however, that the most important way in which children learn these concepts is through their own writing. In the writing conferences we describe with Patrick, George, and Justin in Chapter 4 you will see this demonstrated. Writing is the major context for the learning of the alphabet.

- Read alphabet books together. Start a collection of alphabet books for the book corner, and include them in your home-borrowing program. Here are some titles of alphabet books that we think take an original approach.

  Anno, M. (1974). *Anno's Alphabet*. New York, NY: Thomas Crowell.

  Hague, K. (1984). *Alphabears: An ABC Book*. Illustrated by Michael Hague. New York, NY: Holt Rinehart & Winston.

  Lessac, F. (1989). *Caribbean Alphabet*. London, UK: Macmillan Caribbean.

  Martin, B., & Archambault, J. (1989). *Chicka chicka boom boom*. New York, NY: Simon & Shuster.

  Musgrove, M. (1976). *Ashanti to Zulu: African Traditions*. New York, NY: Dial.

  Owens, M.B. (1988). *A Caribou Alphabet*. Willowdale, ON: Firefly Books.

  Rankin, L. (1991). *The Handmade Alphabet*. New York, NY: Dial.

  Van Allsburg, C. (1987). *The Z Was Zapped*. Boston, MA: Houghton Mifflin.

- Talk about the difference between the name of the letter and the sound that it makes.

- Sing the alphabet song.
- Make a class alphabet to be displayed at children's eye-level. Each child makes one or two pictures illustrating an alphabet letter. Some tips for making alphabets include:

  avoid stereotypical images (e.g., I for Indian);
  use words from the children's vocabulary;
  use photographs of the children and their names to create a truly personal and meaningful alphabet;
  reflect the cultures of your community in your choice of words;
  make alphabets on themes such as food, animals, fairy tales; when choosing illustrations ensure that the sound is accurate. The illustration must represent the sound you want to teach, for example, "top" not "tree" (tree is a blend).

- Make alphabet books with the children using one letter as the focus, for example, "The Book of D." Every child creates a page with a word or sentence using words beginning with D. "David likes dogs." "Diving is dangerous."
- Incorporate learning about letters into interest centers. As an example, a center that displays shells could have a list of words beginning with **sh**.
- Play *Grandmother Went to Market*. The first child in the circle starts off by saying, "Grandmother went to market and she bought some bananas." The second child says, "Grandmother went to market and she bought some bananas and a bear." The next child repeats the first two objects and adds a third. Continue until the list is too long to remember (usually 8-10 items) then change to a new letter.
- When children are lining up or going to activities, organize them by initial letter (e.g., all the people whose names begin with B).
- Tell alphabet stories that help to illustrate the sounds of the consonants. Use traditional rhymes, riddles, and tongue-twisters. Here are some story and rhyme ideas to get you started. Modify them as you like, and substitute the names of children in the class to make them your own. Try inventing stories involving the children in the class and events that they have shared such as field trips. Here are some suggestions for the sorts of stories you can invent.

Alphabet Antics: Stories, Poems, and Tongue Twisters

A Story for B

Brandon and his Dad loved to go fishing together. They had an old motor boat. When they were ready to set off, Dad pulled a handle and the motor spluttered into life. B-B-B-B-B. Then it stopped. Dad pulled again. B-B-B-B-B. It stopped again. Brandon began to be worried. Perhaps they wouldn't be able to go fishing after all. Dad tried again. B-B-B-B-B. This time it worked and the little boat began to move out across the lake. They had a wonderful day together.

A Tongue-Twister for B

Betty bought a bit of butter
But she said "This butter's bitter."
So she bought some better butter.
Traditional

A Story for C and K

(C can be hard and say k as in castle; c can be soft and say s as in ceiling. Start with the k sound.)
One day Carrie and her Mum visited an old castle. A king used to live there a long time ago. It had big rooms and lots of old furniture. In one of the rooms was a very tall clock in a case, with a picture of the sun and the moon on its big face. But the clock was not working. It's pendulum was still. "I want to hear the clock say tick-tock," said Carrie. One of the people who looked after the castle heard Carrie. "The clock needs winding up," he said. "I'll get the key and wind it if you can wait a minute." So Carrie and her Mum waited while the man fetched a great big key. He opened the little door at the front of the clock and put the key into a special keyhole. Then he turned slowly. C-C-C-C-C was the sound as he turned that big key. Then he gave the pendulum a little swing and the clock began to tick TICK-TOCK, TICK-TOCK, TICK-TOCK.

Rhymes for C and K

Tick-tock, tick-tock, goes my grandad's big clock. (said slowly)
But my Mummy's little clock goes tick-tock, tick-tock, tick-tock.
(said very fast)

> Hickory Dickory Dock
> The mouse ran up the clock
> The clock struck one, the mouse ran down
> Hickory Dickory Dock
>
> *Traditional*

A Story for D

When David and his parents went on a camping trip it rained every day. The rain dripped from the trees. D-D-D-D-D. It dripped from the umbrellas D-D-D-D-D and it dripped from the end of David's rain jacket. David lay in bed at night snug and warm in the camper and wished for the rain to stop. He could hear the rain on the roof of the camper dripping, dripping. D-D-D-D-D. Soon David was asleep and he was dreaming that he was marching in a band. He was playing a drum D-D-D-D-D. In the morning when he woke up it was very quiet. He couldn't hear that D-D-D-D-D sound any more. "It's stopped raining!" he shouted and jumped out of bed.

A Story for F

Fiona went to a birthday party and at the party she was given a red balloon, but because she was going home on the bus her friend's mother said, "We won't blow up your balloon Fiona. You can do it yourself when you get home." At the end of the party Fiona said goodbye and thank you for having me. Then she went home on the bus with her balloon. When she got home she tried to blow up the balloon. F-F-F-F-F she went as she blew air into the balloon. It grew big and fat. But before she could tie the end all the air came out F-F-F-F-F, and the balloon was limp and flat. She tried again. F-F-F-F-F. Now the balloon was big again. But she still couldn't get a knot in the end quickly enough. F-F-F-F-F went the balloon as all the air rushed out. Fiona was starting to feel upset when her big sister came along. "I'll help you," she said. Fiona blew air into the balloon. F-F-F-F-F. She held the end while her sister tied the knot.

A Story for G

(Like **c**, **g** has a hard and a soft sound. Teach the hard sound, **g** as in girl before **g** as in bridge.)
A girl called Gaye was visiting the zoo. Her favorite animal was a gorilla named Guy. Guy was walking back and forth, back and forth in his cage. Gaye stopped to look at him. "Hello Guy," she said. Guy gave her a curious look then beat his hands on his big chest. "G-G-G-G-G," he roared!

A Story for H

Hero was a huge yellow dog. He loved to run and jump and go for long walks with his friend Harry. One day they saw a rabbit on a hillside. Hero decided to chase the rabbit. He ran as fast as he could up a very steep hill, but no matter how fast he ran the rabbit was always ahead of him. At last the rabbit reached her burrow and disappeared, safe underground. Hero sat down completely out of breath and panted hard. H-H-H-H. Harry caught up with him and sat down too. He was also panting. H-H-H-H-H. "You've made us both out of breath, Hero. We need to go home for a long drink of water." And so they did.

(H is also HOT on your HAND!)

A Story for J

Jumping Jack had a pogo stick. J-J-J-J-J-J went the stick as he hopped along. The spring was a little squeaky you see.

A Story for L

A lazy lion lay in the sun, his long tongue lolling out of his mouth. Suddenly he heard singing. "L-L-L-L-L," sang a little voice. Lazy lion sat up. "Who is singing?" he asked. "It's me," said a little bird in a tree above his head. "I love to sing. Will you join in with me?" The lion tried to sing L-L-L-L-L, but however hard he tried to he could not make his great big voice say L. A lion can only roar.

A Story for M

A mother was preparing a birthday party. The children kept peeping into the kitchen. "Go away," cried the mother "You can't come in!" All morning the children kept trying to see the birthday treats but the mother would not let them! At last the birthday guests began to arrive and it was tea time. The mother opened the door and there was the birthday table loaded down with the most delicious cakes and cookies that you ever did see. "M-M-M-M-M," said all the children and they sat down to eat. "M-M-M-M-M," they said as they ate the cakes. "M-M-M-M-M," they said as they ate the cookies. "Thank you for the lovely party," they said as they went home. "It was YUMMMMM!"

A Story for N

Nigel put a nut in his nose. He had to go to hospital to have it taken out. It was so horrible he never, never, never put anything in his nose ever again, and neither will you!

A Story for P

Percy did not like peas. Every time his mother gave him peas for dinner Percy would spit them out P-P-P-P-P onto the floor. You wouldn't do such a terrible thing, would you?

A Tongue-Twister for P

>Peter Piper picked a peck of pickled peppers
>If Peter picked a peck of pickled peppers
>Where's the peck of pickled peppers Peter Piper picked?
>
>*Traditional*

A Poem for P

>Sampan
>Waves lap lap
>Fish fins clap clap
>Brown sails flap flap
>Chop-sticks tap tap;
>
>Up and down the long green river,
>Oh hey, oh hey, lanterns quiver,

Willow branches brush the river,
Oh hey, oh hey, lanterns quiver.

Chop sticks tap tap
Brown sails flap flap
Fish fins clap, clap
Waves lap lap.

Anonymous

A Story for Q

Quackers was a little duck. He was learning to talk and learning to fly. All the other ducks said, "Quack, quack," but Quackers could only say "QU-QU-QU-QU-QU." "When will I quack like all the others?" Quackers asked his mother. "One day little duckling," she said. One day a big fox came into the farmyard. No one saw him but Quackers. He was so frightened he didn't know what to do but he was a brave little duck. He stood up and opened his beak. Out came "QU-QU-QU-QU-QUACK!" The fox was so scared he ran away. "I can quack!" said Quackers. Everyone hugged him.

A Story for R

Randy had a red racing car. It roared around the track. It's engine went R-R-R-R-R. It raced across the finish line. It won the race. Hooray!

A Story for S

Sandy was sitting on a log. He saw a long, slippery body come slithering through the grass towards him. It was his friend Sammy the Snake. Sammy saw his friend Sandy. "S-S-S-S-S," said Sammy, which was his way of saying hello. "S-S-S-S-S," said Sandy in reply. And they went off together singing a song.

A Tongue-Twister for S

She sells sea-shells on the sea-shore
If she sells sea-shells on the sea-shore
Where are the sea-shells she sells on the sea-shore?

Traditional

46

A Rhyme for S

Swan swam over the sea;
Swim swan swim.
Swan swam back again,
Well swum swan!

Traditional

A Story for T

A little boy sat on his grandfather's lap and listened to his big pocket watch. "I used to use this when I worked on the railway," said his Grandfather. "It helped me to keep the trains running on time." The old railway watch had a sound like this that you could only hear if you put it up to your ear very closely: T-T-T-T-T.

A Story for V

High in the sky an airplane was flying. Vera could just hear the sound of its engine. V-V-V-V-V was the noise; a low hum in the distance. She looked up and all she could see was a V shape in the sky. "I wonder where it is going," thought Vera. "Is it going very far away? Who is on the plane? Where are they going?" Then the V-V-V-V-V sound was gone and the plane was out of sight.

A Poem for W

White-capped waves are washing
On the wintry shore
Waves that wander where they will
While the wild winds roar

A Story for Z

Zack lay on his tummy watching the bees go in and out of the hive. Z-Z-Z-Z-Z went the bees. "They are looking for pollen in the flowers," said his Grandfather. "They make it into honey."

The Developing Reader and Writer

Whole-class and small-group demonstrations continue to be an important part of introducing children to the ways in which print represents meanings. As with Beginning Readers, whole-class meetings should be relatively short. Small-group meetings should be addressed to those who need the information. For best results, keep the groups small (4-5 children) so all can have a role. Thinking aloud or modeling what you are doing as you read and write is the best way to demonstrate how the reading and writing process works. As you read a story or generate a written message, talk your way through the process.

Useful Things to Know about Phonics

The following list details facts about phonics that Developing Readers may find helpful. Introduce these points when they are needed and show how they can be used to unlock words. Remember, phonics rules are not the curriculum; reading is the curriculum and phonics are a tool for reading. There are too many rules to learn them all and too many exceptions to every rule. It is not necessary for children to be drilled in the rules, or to be able to repeat them. It is very important to be flexible, and to understand that in sounding out using phonics there are many traps for the unwary reader. Phonic clues should be used together with meaning clues to find a word that makes sense.

- The most powerful phonic clue for unlocking an unknown word is the first letter.
- Consonants can blend together to make one sound. Consonant blends are: **bl, br, cl, cr, dr, fl, fr, gl, gr, pl, pr, sc, sl, sm, sn, sp, sr, st, sw, scr, spl, squ, str, thr, nd, nk, ng, nt, ft.** It is important to be able to blend and to hear blends in words. Together with consonants, consonant blends form the onsets to all words.
- **Onsets** and **rimes** are a useful form of word analysis. These are units somewhere between the phoneme and the syllable. The onset is that part of a syllable that comes before the vowel. It will be a consonant or a consonant blend. The rime is everything else. As an example, in ''sit'' **s** is the onset and **it** is the rime. In ''split'' **spl** is the onset and **it** is the rime. There is evidence that children are better able to identify the spelling

of whole rimes than of individual vowel sounds. They seem to have a psychological reality that makes better sense to children than phonemes alone. There are nearly 500 words that can be generated using just 37 rimes (Adams, 1990, p. 84):

ack, ain, ake, ale, all, ame, an, ank, ap, ash, at, ate, aw, ay eat, ell, est, ice, ick, ide, ight, ill, in, ine, ing, ink, ip, ir, ock, oke, op, or, ore, uck, ug, ump, unk.

Word families can be built using these rimes. When children learn a rime they can apply it in new words. If you know **all** in "ball" then you can also read it in "fall" and "tall." Phonics patterns remain stable within these rimes, so there is some purpose in teaching them as tools for word attack.

- When a vowel comes between two consonants, it usually has a short vowel sound (about 60% of the time), for example, cat, ran, bet, pen, sit, win, pot, mop, hut, sun. Teach these as onsets and rimes; that is, as part of word families. Although they are best learned in rhymes where they occur naturally, we have suggested games to help children become proficient at recognizing rimes (see Phonics Wheels, p. 110).

- "When two vowels go walking the first one does the talking." This refers to the generalization that when two vowels come together in a word, the first vowel is long and the second is silent. The first vowel says its name. This is usually valid for **ee, oa,** and **ay**, and about two-thirds of the time for **ea** and **ai** (e.g., sheet, boat, day, meat, rain), but is unreliable for **ei, ie,** or **oo**. It is not valid for diphthongs (glided vowel sounds) represented by **oi, oy, ou,** and **ow** (e.g., oil, boy, out, cow). In other words, the rule only has about 45 per cent utility. The large number of exceptions to the rule suggest that a more useful way to approach word attack is through onsets and rimes. Learn rimes such as **oat, eet, eat, ay, ain, oot, ook, ound, out, owl, oil**, and see how many words can be built. You can read an unknown word by analogy if you can find a known word with the same rime. For example, if a child is hesitating at the word "sentence" she might be able to read **ten** and then to see that **sen** has the same pattern. If she can read "fence" then she can also read **tence**. Developing word attack strategies that utilize knowledge of rimes is most useful but children should also be taught that these families have their exceptions (e.g., done, one) so the best clue to pronunciation is to see the word in the context of the sentence in which it appears.

- When two vowels appear in a word and one is an **e** at the end of the word, the first vowel is generally long and the final **e** is silent. The "magic-e" makes the vowel say its name about 60 per cent of the time (e.g., cake, hope, shape, kite). Again, the teaching of onsets and rimes will help in the recognition of these words.
- When there is only one vowel in a word or syllable and it comes at the end of the syllable or word, it is usually long (e.g., be, go, my).
- Vowels that appear before the letter **r** are affected by the **r** sound. Look at the rimes in these words: car, care, her, here, girl, wire, horn, short, fur, turn, picture. This is another series of word families that can be explored.
- The letter **c** can be hard or soft. In general, it is hard (like **k**) when followed by **a, o**, or **u** (e.g., cat, coat, candle). It is soft (like **s**) when followed by **e, i**, or **y** (e.g., ceiling, bicycle, circus).
- The letter **g** can be hard or soft. In general, it is hard (e.g., go, get, garden) when followed by **a, o**, or **u**. It is soft (like **j**) when it is followed by **e, i,** or **y** (e.g., giant, giraffe, gym).

Ideas for Demonstrations

Read Aloud from Big Books and Charts (Shared Reading)

- Use lots of poetry and rhyme. A poem a week can be shared together, posted on the wall, and copied by children into handwriting books. An alternative is to give the children a copy of the poem to stick in a scrapbook. They love to take these home to read to their families. Use a copy of the poem to identify words that belong to the same word family by coloring the rimes.
- Learn some of the traditional songs like "Old McDonald Had a Farm," "She'll Be Coming Round the Mountain," and "Six Little Ducks" using the big book format. These can be a springboard for small groups to print and illustrate their favorite song and perform it for their friends. Point out families of words in the songs — words that share the same spelling pattern (have the same rime), such as make, bake, take.

Teach Strategies for Unlocking Print

- Talk about the process of reading, and show how to use contextual, syntactic, and phonic clues. Demonstrate how to unlock an unknown word. What clues are there? Where can we try? What else can we do? We can:
  guess from the picture;
  guess from the sense of the story;
  guess from the sense of the sentence;
  guess from these, *and* the first letter of the word;
  guess from the structure of the word, break it into syllables;
  look for a small word within the big word, use our knowledge of word families to work out an unknown word by analogy with one we know;
  go back to the beginning of the sentence and start again;
  go on to the end of the sentence and come back to it.

Teach Strategies for Reading Non-Fiction

- Use non-fiction text, as well as stories and rhymes. Read aloud from books that are related to themes in science and social studies. Begin to introduce the children to some of the features of non-narrative writing using big books. Point out the use of headings, indexes, and how diagrams are used to explain information. Showing the children how a book is laid out so that we can find information helps them to construct projects clearly, using diagrams, labels, etc.
- Teach the children how to access their prior knowledge before reading. Read the title of a book or article. Ask everyone to write the facts they think might be in the book using a web or a list. The children can indicate which ones they are sure about and which ones they are unsure about. Read the information and note when facts confirm the predictions. Ask the children what additional information came up that wasn't anticipated.
- Generate questions about a topic prior to the reading. What do you want to know? What do you wonder about? After the reading, see how many questions were answered. What questions remain unanswered? What have we learned by reading this book? What information was the most interesting, unusual, or surprising?

- Make labels for displays at science, math, and social studies centers.
- Label children's work.
- Create written instructions for activity centers.
- Talk about word choices.
- Talk about spelling patterns.
- Point out word families — make connections between words that have the same rime.
- Point out punctuation marks and explain their function — periods, capital letters, question marks, exclamation marks, speech marks.

The Fluent Reader and Writer in the Early Years

Lucy McCormick Calkins uses the term mini-lessons for short lessons that take a single point and demonstrate it clearly. Fluent readers and writers continue to need demonstrations of this sort even though they are more independent in reading and writing. We have found that mini-lessons in reading help the children learn about writing and writers while mini-lessons in writing help them to become more efficient readers because they learn more about spelling patterns, punctuation, and grammatical structures of the language. Reading and writing are not treated as two separate subjects: workshop time is as long as possible so that all manner of reading and writing activities can take place, including direct instruction or mini-lessons, conferences, and lots of time for the children to read, write, and research.

We continue to instruct in small groups according to need and to offer versions of mini-lessons to individuals during conferences. We also give quick lessons to the whole class to introduce key concepts and procedures that everyone needs to be aware of. As an example, we might teach everyone about the correct use of capital letters to start a new sentence. Those children who are showing that they are ready to do this consistently in their writing might be brought together for another lesson that reinforces the concept. Later, in a writing conference, one of these children might be shown again how to capitalize, and would set this skill as a goal at the back of his writing folder. When he is using capitals correctly to start his sentences, the goal moves to another list and becomes one of the things he knows about writing.

Since it is important that the children can talk about the skills they are learning and see their own progress we need to set goals during conferences. Our mini-lessons provide suggestions for "Things I Am Learning About Writing." It is satisfying to children when they can transfer these to the list of "Things I Know About Writing." These skills lists demonstrate to parents the scope of a child's achievement during the year. Start the year by organizing your writing folders so that they include lists of goals and skills that have been mastered. Keep the list of "Things I Am Learning" shorter than the list of "Things I Know."

Our reading-writing classroom begins with a whole-class activity; a story shared and a mini-lesson often arising from the story. The children move into reading and writing tasks, and we hold small-group mini-lessons and conferences with individuals. At the end of the lesson a sharing time gives children a chance to show their work to an appreciative audience and brings closure. Sometimes it is appropriate to refer back to the mini-lesson of the day during this time. "I really think Shane was thinking hard about using capital letters at the start of all his sentences!"

Mini-Lesson Ideas for Reading and Spelling

Choosing a Book for Independent Reading

Children who can read may need help in learning how to make good choices in the library. Some tend to choose books that are too long and difficult for them while others choose to read easy material and never stretch themselves unless helped to take a risk. To get the most from reading children should be working with text that they can read with 93-98 per cent accuracy. Show them how to:

• read the blurb on the cover to see if the story appeals to them;
• look at the number of pages — how long will it take to read this book?
• read the first page — how often do they have to stop to work out what a word says? If they stop for more than five words on a page then the book is too difficult;
• find books by their favorite authors in the library.

A good read should challenge the reader to think about what

they are reading but not present obstacles to understanding. Tell the children it is okay to abandon a book they don't like — all readers do this.

Monitoring Personal Reading

Independent readers need to be aware of their reading habits. Do they skip read when a word is difficult? Do they stop and sound it out? Can they break it into syllables? Do they use a dictionary to check the meanings of words that puzzle them? Do they stop and self-correct when they have lost the meaning? How do they ensure that they understand what they are reading? Children should be encouraged to stop and work out words they don't understand.

Mini-lessons can help reinforce good reading techniques.

- Is the meaning clear? What can they do if they are lost? Ask them to go back and re-read the paragraph, stopping on words that puzzle them. They can use their skills of prediction. What has happened so far? What would make sense here? Use knowledge of phonics to sound out words. Use knowledge of word families to find an unknown word by analogy with one they do know. If they don't know what a word sounds like, they can ask someone.
- Show how to use a dictionary to look up the meaning of a word. This involves knowing how to use alphabetical order, which can be a separate mini-lesson.
- Ask the children to keep a list of new and exciting words. Every book will introduce new vocabulary. Have the children become conscious of new words as they meet them. Start a class list that children can add to as they discover new and unusual words. These words can be discussed at sharing time.
- It is helpful to think about what you already know about a topic before you start reading about it. Show the children how to make a web of ideas on a topic, which will alert them to the vocabulary that will probably come up in the reading.

Using Phonics to Help Reading and Spelling

Phonic rules and generalizations are not a substitute for direct practice with words in context and they are of temporary value. Some of the more unusual phonic configurations, however, may be of interest to young fluent readers and will certainly help them in decoding unknown and difficult words. These mini-lessons will also help with spelling and are more useful in teaching spelling patterns than in reading. Keep the mini-lessons brief, and embed them in the context of real reading activities. Show how to use the phonics to see spelling patterns and to unlock troublesome words. Children can keep a "Spelling Notebook" in which they collect words belonging to families or conforming to rules. Using the mini-lesson format, it is possible to introduce strategies for efficient reading that children can apply during guided reading (with you) and independent reading. You can refer to mini-lessons during individual reading-writing conferences. Your goal is to enable the children to use the strategies independently so that they can understand what they read, pronounce new words accurately, and add new words to their oral and written vocabulary.

Here are some mini-lesson topics for spelling:

- The rules governing hard and soft **c** and **g**: (face, space, ice, rice, nice, slice, twice, voice, ceiling, palace, lettuce, cent, accident, dance, circle, city, circus, pencil, bicycle, sauce; orange, cabbage, bridge, badge, cage, giant, age, stage, large, page, hinge, ranger, ginger, germ, village, etc.). Start a collection and post it in a chart.
- **Ph** as in photograph, telephone, alphabet, nephew, phrase, elephant, orphan, etc. Start a collection of **ph** words, which sound like **f**.
- Silent letters: **k**, as in knock, knight, know, knew, knee, knob, knife, etc. Try some Knock Knock jokes! (Knock Knock. Who's there? Amos. Amos who? A mosquito just bit you.); **w** as in write, wrong, wring, wrap, wrist, wreck; **g** as in gnome, gnash, gnat, gnarled, gnaw.
- **Ight** as in night, fight, light, tonight, might.

> Star light, star bright
> First star I see tonight.
> I wish I may, I wish I might,
> Have the wish I wish tonight.
>
> *Traditional*

- Vowels affected by R:
  ar: car, tar, far, star, farm.
  er: This sound often comes at the end of a word, changing a

noun into one who does an action. Occupations, then, usually end in **er**. Farm-farmer, work-worker, paint-painter. It also expresses the comparative as in big-bigger, fast-faster.

ir: girl, whirl, twirl, first, thirst, bird, third, chirp, shirt, thirty.

or: story, short, for, store, horse, corn, fork, pork, cork.

ur: burn, turn, curl, hurl, church, lurch, fur, hurt.

- **Y** at the end of words when it makes the sound "ee."

> Spring is
> Showery, flowery, bowery.
> Summer is
> hoppy, croppy, poppy.
> Autumn is
> wheezy, sneezy, freezy.
> Winter is
> slippy, drippy, nippy.
>
> *Traditional*

- Suffixes:

ful: The suffix **ful** means full of, or overflowing with, for example, wonderful, beautiful, careful, thankful. When words end in **y**, drop the **y** and add an **i** as in beauty-beautiful.

ly: adjectives that end with a consonant change into adverbs with the addition of **ly**, for example, silently, quickly, badly, suddenly. Adjectives that end in **y** drop the **y** and add **i** before the **ly** ending, for example, happily, merrily, tidily.

ness: **y** changes to **i** when **ness** is added to a root word, for example, laziness, happiness, tidiness. The suffix means "the state of being."

less: when this suffix is added to a root word, the meaning is "without," for example, blameless means without blame. Other examples are shapeless, heartless, homeless, painless.

able: though it looks like the word "able," the suffix is pronounced differently, for example, laughable, adorable, changeable, agreeable, valuable. Like **ness**, **able** refers to a state of being.

ment: the sound of this suffix is not a short **e** vowel, but a sort of swallowed sound. The emphasis is not on the last syllable, for example, advertisement, improvement, pavement, movement, government — **ment** changes a verb into a noun; to advertise-an advertisement; to govern-a government.

tion: although some words spell this sound with **tian, cian, sion, cean,** and even **chion**, in 90 per cent of cases a word ending in **shun** will be spelled **tion**. Here are some words to start

56

a collection: nation, station, election, action, suggestion, question, vacation, construction, relations, participation, operation.

ing: the infinite form or root of a verb is changed into the present continuous by the addition of **ing**, but this changes the spelling for those words that end in consonants. The final consonant must be doubled, for example, run-running, stop-stopping, rub-rubbing. Watch for exceptions like hear-hearing, roar-roaring, cry-crying, speak-speaking.

ed: the addition of **ed** to a verb changes the infinite form or root into the past tense. As with **ing** this changes the spelling of words that end in consonants. These must be doubled, for example, stop-stopped, rub-rubbed, walk-walked.

- Prefixes

Prefixes may give a clue as to the meaning of a word. The origins of many of our prefixes in English are from Latin. However, morphological analysis of words can lead to difficulties because in many cases the entire word is better known than the "root." In the examples that follow, if you strip the prefixes you are left, in some cases, with meaningless words or words that then mean something completely different. Watch out for the words where the prefix is an integral part of the whole word, like exhale and explode.

un: **un** means not and can be placed at the beginning of other words to change their meanings. Through discussion of words beginning with **un**, children will see that its addition produces a word of opposite meaning, for example, kind-unkind, like-unlike, happy-unhappy, load-unload, pack-unpack, zip-unzip.

in: this prefix can sometimes mean in or into, for example, indoors, inside, infield, inland, income. It can also mean not, for example, incorrect, inexpensive, invisible, inconsiderate.

mis: the meaning that this prefix brings to a word is wrong or bad, for example, adventure-misadventure, spell-misspell.

ex: the meaning of this prefix is out, or out of; for example, exhale, explain, express, explore, explode, exhibit, exit, exclaim.

dis: this can mean not, as in dislike, disagree, displease, dishonest, distrustful. It can mean apart, as in dislodge, displace, disengage, disappear. It can also mean the opposite of the root word, as in disconnect, discolor, disown.

Dividing Words into Syllables

There are some rules for syllabilization that seem complicated, but will be developed inductively by most children. Here are the rules for those who will benefit by more explicit help in dividing words so they may see the small words within the big words. Do not teach the rules for their own sake, but as a strategy for word-attack.

- Have the children look at this list of words: ask, with, but, off, and, in, end, flip, rob, jump, up, stop. The words end in a consonant and they have only one vowel. The vowel sound is short. Now look at this list: by, fly, she, he, no, go, so, we. The words end in a vowel and the sound is long. This generalization works well when dividing a long word into syllables. When the syllable ends in a consonant, the preceding vowel will be short, for example, sing-er, ask-ing, but-ter, sis-ter. When the syllable ends in a vowel, the vowel sound will be long, for example, ti-ger, pu-pil, di-no-saur.
- As every syllable contains a vowel sound, the number of syllables in a word will be determined by the number of vowel sounds, for example, el-e-phant, di-no-saur, mount-ain.
- If two or more consonants follow a vowel the word is usually divided between the consonants, for example, bet-ter, run-ning, rab-bit.
- Prefixes and suffixes are usually separate syllables, for example, in-vite, dis-like.
- The consonant preceding **le** joins with it to make a syllable, for example, ta-ble, mar-ble, spar-kle, bee-tle.
- The suffix **ed** forms a separate syllable when the root word ends in **d** or **t**, for example, heat-ed, want-ed. Otherwise the **ed** combines with the vowel to make a single syllable, for example, hoped, pecked, rubbed.

Mini-Lesson Ideas for Responding to Reading

Using a Reading Journal

Fluent Readers do not need to read aloud to you often, but you do need to know what sense they are making of what they are reading. A reading journal is one way for you to interact with children about books. Children write as they read, questioning and reflecting upon the story as it unfolds. They write a few thoughts at the end of each reading period. If they are reading a novel, they will write approximately every ten pages. If they are reading a picture book, it is more likely that they will use the journal to sum up what the book was about and to offer an opinion about it. The following mini-lessons teach about responding to books and also teach children about writing stories, helping them to uncover what it is that makes a story successful. The authors of good children's books are the best teachers!

What Makes a Good Entry?

Show what an interesting journal entry looks like. Use an overhead, the chalk board, or chart paper. Consider developing a joint response with the class or use a child's writing with permission. "I liked it. It was good" doesn't tell us very much. We want children to write about what they liked and why — what intrigued them, caught their interest, excited them, made them laugh? Their ideas are important. It's not so much a quest for the "right answer" to the question as a means of exploring what the reader finds important. This is sometimes hard for children who have been trained to fill in the blanks and get the answers right. They need to be encouraged to write their own ideas.

Asking Questions

Show how you can use a journal to ask questions and wonder about the story. Why did the characters do, say, or feel what they did? What will happen next? Why? Discuss predictions. What are they based on? Are we right or does the story take an unexpected twist?

Characterization

Talk about characters. Who is the "main character?" How do we know? What makes this character different from the others? How is she or he described? How does she or he behave? Do you like this character? Would you want to be friends with him or her? *Amazing Grace* by Mary Hoffman is a wonderful picture book for discussing character. Grace is talented, lively, and determined to be Peter Pan in the school play, but is faced with prejudice from other children because of her black skin and her gender. She wins the part and "was an amazing Peter Pan," because, as her Nana says, "If Grace puts her mind to it, she can do anything she want."

A Sense of Place

Talk about settings. What is the importance of place in a story? How do writers describe places? How does this help to set the mood of a story? What sort of words are used to describe the place? (Can we add any to our word collections?) Here is a description from Ursula LeGuin's *Catwings*. How does it help us to understand why Mrs. Tabby makes her children leave home?

"It really was a terrible neighborhood and getting worse. Car wheels and truck wheels rolling past all day — rubbish and litter — hungry dogs — endless shoes and boots walking, running, stamping, kicking — nowhere safe and quiet, and less and less to eat. Most of the sparrows had moved away. The rats were fierce and dangerous; the mice were scrawny."

Openings

Talk about how the story opens. Is it a strong opening? Does it make you want to read on? How does the writer capture our attention? Consider this opening by Ted Hughes to his book, *The Iron Man*.

"The Iron Man came to the top of the cliff. How far had he walked? Nobody knows. Where had he come from? Nobody knows. How was he made? Nobody knows.

Taller than a house, the Iron Man stood at the top of the cliff, on the very brink, in the darkness."

Endings

Talk about endings. Does the book conclude in a satisfying way? Do you like the way it ends? Are you satisfied that the story ends this way? *Catwings* ends like this:

"Oh Hank," Susan whispered, "their wings are furry."
"Oh, James," Harriet whispered, "their hands are kind."

At last the cats have found a place of safety and have found human beings with kind hands. The parallel structure adds to our appreciation of the contentment of the cats and the children.

Personal Connections

Did the book remind you of anything that has happened to you? Can you make connections between personal stories and those in books? Can you empathize with the situations in which the characters find themselves? Do you know what it felt like to be Grace, determined to get what she wants, despite the opinion of others? Do you know how the Catwings felt, looking for a home? The measure of a good read is in how much it draws us into the story so that we become absorbed.

Titles

What's in a title? How do writers choose them? We can ask all kinds of questions about titles. It is an exciting moment when children choose titles for stories they have written. A good mini-lesson is to take a number of books that the children are familiar with and classify the titles. Some are named for the main character, some give a hint about the plot, some ask questions, and some are exclamations. How will the children choose the title for their next story?

Procedures

How often do you want children to write in their journals? What about the questions you ask? Are the children answering them? How do you want them to lay out an entry on the page? A clear heading, including the title of the book and the date for each entry, is important. An occasional mini-lesson on how to format entries is useful.

Other Responses to Literature

There are numerous follow-ups that children can do in response to a book that they have read. Using writing, drawing, and drama they can describe, re-enact, and extend their interpretation of a story in many ways. Literary sociograms, story completions, character portraits, new book covers, and character report cards are just a few of the response ideas that you can choose from. The following titles are good reference books full of sound ideas for response strategies.

Johnson, T., & Daphne, L. (1987). *Literacy Through Literature*. Richmond Hill, ON: Scholastic.

Cairney, T. *Other Worlds: The Endless Possibilities*. Portsmouth, NH: Heinemann.

Harste, J., Burke, C., & Short, K. (1988). *Creating Classrooms for Authors: Reading-Writing Connections*. Portsmouth, NH: Heinemann.

Introduce the procedures for doing a response strategy in mini-lessons. Everyone needs the demonstration of how to do it and what it involves. Later, the children begin to choose the response they think best fits the book they have read.

Researching a Topic

Mini-lessons are needed to help children with the following skills:

Locating Information in the Library

How does the card index, microfiche, or computer work? You will need to team up with the teacher-librarian to ensure that children are given an opportunity to learn about the way the library operates.

Finding Information in a Book

Teach children how to use a table of contents and an index. It involves understanding the principle of alphabetization so a mini-lesson on this can save time for children who are starting their research projects.

Making Notes

Once the children have found the information, they have to record it in a way that will make sense later. There are many ways to take notes. Children can learn how to make webs, lists, and notes under headings. The temptation for children is to copy out the words in the book so it is important to help them to read and then jot down important ideas in phrases and single words, not in sentences. This helps when they come to write text because the information must be in their words, not in those of the source material. Some whole-class experiences around reading a piece of information, making point-form notes, and then writing it up is necessary before children tackle individualized projects.

Organizing Information

One idea for organizing information is to jot down key words and concepts from the source books on individual slips of paper. Let's say we are researching butterflies. We find words like flowers, pollen, stamens, wings, antennae, pupa, caterpillar, leaves, and so on. These words are then sorted into categories under headings — description, life cycle, food, enemies, etc. and pasted onto lists on large sheets of paper. The act of sorting is a wonderful way to consolidate the learning. The children decide on the categories. Each list becomes the topic for a paragraph in the final report.

Revising Writing

Revising, the stage in the writing process when writers make changes in structure to their initial drafts, may include adding or deleting words, phrases, sentences, and paragraphs, and changing the order of the text. Young children are unlikely to engage in much content revision. Their writing flows so naturally and sounds so much like their speech that it is unnecessary to change the structure for better effect. They are also reluctant to change things because they make them the way they want them in the first place. Gradually, however, through mini-lessons and conferences, young writers can begin to see how the addition of more information can help enrich a story, or how adding words that describe things in more detail can make a piece come to life. Accepting the suggestions of others for improving a piece of writing is a major developmental milestone and one we watch for closely. In mini-lessons we like to model:

- how to hold a writing conference with a friend. We role play ways to respond to writing — the sorts of questions and suggestions a friend can ask and make that are useful to writers.

- how to hear the sound of personal writing by reading it aloud to oneself (author's mumble).
- how to make revisions by cutting and pasting work, using arrows, extra bits of paper, and carats. Because we are teaching the early stages of revision at this point, we like the children to work on loose sheets of paper that can be cut and pasted and moved around. Paper clips and folders are an essential part of this organization.

Editing Writing

Editing or proofreading, which takes place after revision, is part of the process of completing a piece of writing. It is the stage of the writing process when we tidy up the piece, correct spelling, punctuation, and grammatical structures. Before children can edit their work successfully, they need to be introduced to the skills of editing and to learn about grammar and punctuation so they can apply this knowledge in their work as editors.

One successful mini-lesson format is to present an unedited piece of writing on an overhead and go through the process of editing with the children. Concentrate on one skill at a time and don't try to do everything in one piece. Here are the basic skills that young writers need to be able to apply in editing. We have divided this list into three topics: punctuation, grammar, and spelling rules. Create your own mini-lessons around these topics, one at a time, and introduce them to children when you see a need.

Punctuation

- The period is sometimes called a full-stop, and that name conveys more of its meaning. It is used when a sentence has ended; the idea has come to a full-stop.
- Capital letters are used at the start of every new sentence and for the names of people and places.
- Question marks signal that a sentence asks a question.
- Exclamation marks show surprise or express excitement.
- Quotation marks surround the language of dialogue. If a character in a story says something, the spoken words are enclosed by speech marks, for example, ''I really like these mini-lessons,'' said the teacher.

- The apostrophe is used to show possession, for example, The children's teacher read a story. You can check to see if you've got it right by reversing the two nouns and inserting "of" — The teacher of the children read a story. When a plural ends in **s** the apostrophe follows the **s** rather than preceding it. (The dogs' favorite toy was a ball.)
- The apostrophe is also used to mark a contraction. The rule for this is consistent so children shouldn't have the trouble they seem to have! If letters are missed when two words are spoken as if they were one, or contracted, then the apostrophe is inserted in place of the letters. To check if an apostrophe is needed, say the two words, for example, There's – There is; I've – I have.

*The full use of the apostrophe and of commas, colons, and semicolons is usually beyond the scope of the primary classroom. Children will encounter them as they progress through the grades.

Grammar

The way we speak and the way we write are different. There is a formality about written English that is absent from the way we talk with our "ums" and "ers," false starts and unfinished sentences. Also, we speak dialects of English that reflect where we live. When children become more comfortable with writing and can read fluently, point out the differences between the way we speak and the way we write. Without suggesting that local speech patterns are "wrong" or inferior, we need to show children that standard written English conforms to certain rules.

We need to help children to construct ideas in sentences that:

- have verbs;
- have agreement between subject and verb;
- are divided by periods and not joined together in an endless string of "and thens."

Children like to learn the names of parts of speech and should develop familiarity with the terms noun, verb, adjective, adverb, and pronoun. These words are useful in talking about writing. They are part of the vocabulary that we need when we discuss writing. If we want to help children to enrich their descriptions by using adjectives, for example, we need to be able to refer to what an adjective is. We can teach these names in mini-lessons, and refer to them in editing conferences. For the sake of clarity, the following definitions can be used in primary classrooms.

- A noun is a word that names places, people, and things (e.g., dog, hat, car).
- A proper noun names places and people. It takes a capital letter (e.g., New York, London, Toronto, King Arthur).
- A collective noun describes a group of things (e.g., gaggle of geese, flock of starlings).
- A verb is a word that describes an action (e.g., sing, run, write).
- An adjective modifies a noun — it tells you more about it (e.g., fierce dog, funny hat, fast car).
- An adverb modifies a verb — it gives more information about the action (e.g., singing sweetly, running quickly).
- A pronoun refers to people and objects already mentioned in a sentence. Pronouns — I, me, you, he, she, it, they — stand in for a noun. Possessive pronouns show belonging: my, mine, his, hers, their, theirs, you, your, yours.

A useful set of books about the parts of speech has been written and illustrated by Ruth Heller. These gorgeous picture books make learning the names of the parts of speech enjoyable.
A Cache of Jewels and other Collective Nouns
Many Luscious Lollipops: A Book About Adjectives
Kites Sail High: A Book About Verbs
Merry-Go-Round: A Book About Nouns
Published by Sandcastle Books, A Division of the Putnam & Grosset Group, New York.

Making Plurals

Most words in English change from singular to plural with the addition of an **s** or **es** but there are some exceptions. Here are the rules for forming the plural.

- Add **s** to most words to make them plural.
- Add **es** to most words that end in **s, z, x, ch,** and **sh** to make them plural (e.g., boxes, ashes, coaches, buses, watches).
- In words that end with a consonant before **y**, change the **y** to **i** and add **es** to form the plural (e.g., community-communities, berry-berries, spy-spies).

- Add **es** to words that end in **o** (e.g., potatoes, tomatoes, heroes).
- Words that end in **f** or **fe** might change to **v** (e.g., wive-wives, knife-knives).

Show the children how to find the plural of a word in the dictionary. Have fun hunting out irregular plurals like woman-women, sheep-sheep, moose-moose, foot-feet, and cactus-cacti.

Spelling

We have listed some of the phonics that help with spelling. Spelling mini-lessons are an integral part of the writing workshop; there are three sources of ideas for constructing your lessons.

1. When you notice that children need to learn something: if a number of children make the same error or ask the same questions, then it is the time to tell them what they need to know.
2. When a project demands that certain words be used by everyone: classroom themes will often dictate the content of your spelling mini-lessons.
3. Things about spelling that you want the children to know: keep a list and check them off once you have dealt with something. You can see at a glance which skills you have covered. Remember, just because you have done it once does not mean that the children have learned it, but it does help in conferences to refer back to the mini-lessons.

A word book in which they write new words and frequently spelled words will be useful to children once they have begun to write about 50 per cent of words in standard spelling in a piece of writing. It is counterproductive to introduce the use of word books too soon because children will lose confidence in their spelling and the flow of their writing will stop. We suggest that they be used after a piece of writing is written, as part of the editing process, rather than as part of the composition process. Make a notebook, one for each child, that has pages cut to create an alphabetical index. Use a mini-lesson to teach the procedure for adding new words to the book and using them in editing. This book replaces the system of writing words on the front of the folder that we used with children at the developing stage.

There are a number of useful books on spelling that can help you to create an integrated spelling program. We recommend:

Phenix, J., & Scott-Dunne, D. (1991). *Spelling Instruction That Makes Sense*. Markham, ON: Pembroke Publishers.

Buchanan, E. (1989). *Spelling for Whole Language Classrooms*. Winnipeg, MB: Whole Language Consultants.

Booth, David. (Ed.). (1991). *Spelling Links*. Markham, ON: Pembroke Publishers.

Publishing Writing

There are lots of ways to present the finished product when a piece of writing is ready for its audience. It can be bound into a book, made into a scroll, pasted onto a card, or presented in many wonderful and creative ways. We like to show the children some of the possibilities and then let them choose. We can discover some of the features of a finished book that we need to include by looking at the books we have in our classrooms. Mini-lessons on publishing include:

- about the author — short biographies found on book jackets. What kind of information do we find out about authors? Examine the "About the Author" information on the back cover of the books in the book corner. What does it tell about the author? Make a list.
- synopses — how does the publisher whet our appetite for the book? Read the "blurb" on the back of a book. Create a similar passage advertising a book the class has heard read aloud.
- publishing information — copyright date, place, author information.
- lists of other books by the same author.
- title pages — What do they look like? What information do they contain?
- end-papers — These are the inside cover of a picture book. What are they like? Look at picture books by artists such as Anthony Browne and Lynn Cherry to see the potential for interesting end-papers. What symbols from the story appear on the end pages? Does the color have any significance?
- illustrations — How are they organized? Is there one for every page? What kinds of different lay-outs can we find? Do they have borders? If yes, what kinds? Some artists who offer a wealth of visual information from which children can learn about illustration techniques are Don and Audrey Woods, Chris Van Allsburg, Errol Le Cain, Fiona French, and Lois Ehlert.

CHAPTER FOUR

Ideas for Responding to the Children

The daily one-on-one conversations that we have with children around their work, whether finished or in progress, are the most crucial of our teaching interactions. We need these times to listen to what the children are saying, to hear their questions, and to find out what is interesting to them, what confuses them, and where they need help. We may help them to plan a piece of work; we may be present during the process of reading or writing and so help with the construction of meaning; or we may respond to the child's finished product. Whatever the context, our responses are important — they must show genuine interest and give appropriate positive reinforcement.

It is often best to let the children talk first and to listen carefully to what they say before we talk. If we are careful listeners, we will learn much about the children's interests, strengths, and knowledge. These interactions show us what skills are being learned and which ones still need to be worked on. What is the children's attitude to reading and writing? Are they happy, enthusiastic, and confident, or reluctant and uncertain? Conferences allow us to find the information we need to make informed judgments about a child's needs. What we teach next depends about on what we see and hear during these times.

Sometimes conferences are short — a child asks a question and we give a response. Sometimes they are more formal — we timetable an opportunity to see every child and we make notes and jot down comments in our record books. We may use the conference time to demonstrate a particular point about language.

Conferences serve as the setting for the most appropriate direct teaching: the teachable moment is that instant when a child needs to know something to get a job done and it often occurs when we are conferencing. We have included some scenarios to illustrate how we conference and respond to children's work in reading and writing.

Conferencing with the Beginning Reader and Writer

Scene 1. Patrick

Patrick is six years old. He wrote this piece without help during the first week of grade one. The children were asked to write about anything they liked — Patrick took the instruction literally!

PATRICK K

ILKPC

ILKBMCILKPC

Looking at this and his big grin, I know that Patrick is proud of what he has accomplished. His letters are all capitals and he is using only letters to represent the sounds he hears in words. Each word is separated from the others by spaces and I can read what he has written. "I like apples. I like pears. I like bananas." Patrick can read it too, and he does so confidently. Before he puts this in his writing folder I have to decide how to respond to the writing. Shall I work on the fact that the sentences are stilted and we could find out much more about what Patrick likes and why he chose to write about fruit if we had a little conversation about it? Shall I focus on the spelling of the words and show Patrick that S makes a **sss** sound, which he needs in the spelling of apples, pears, and bananas? This is early in the year and I don't know Patrick well. He seems confident, but I don't want to push him to do more writing than he feels like at the moment. He seems to have experience of the sort of language that appears in early readers so maybe he thinks that this is what writing in school ought to sound like. We can work on enriching his sentences later. I talk with Patrick about fruit and which of these is his favorite. We discuss the fact that he can write his name and that his mother showed him how. I decide that he is well on the way to sorting out which letter makes which sound so I show him how to form the letter S. "Guess what? We have this letter to make an **s** sound as well as this one, C. Can you see any S letters around the room?" Patrick finds the S for Snail on the alphabet chart and points to it. "Yes, and you look for words that start with S. Let me know when you find some more." Patrick puts his writing away and I make a note of what we have worked on in my record book.

Sept. 3. Spelling phonetic — one or two letters per word. Not sure of all 26. Worked on S. Needs encouragement to use richer language.

Scene 2. George

As I enter the dramatic play center, an area that is now a thriving pizza parlor, I am met by five-year-old George. "What'll you have?" he asks. As I place my order "A small pizza with onions and tomatoes," George records it on his pad.

He then hurries away to place my order with the cook. When he returns I ask him if my order is correct. He looks on his pad and reads, ''One pizza with tomatoes and onions that's small.''

This shows me that George knows that writing is talk written down. His writing shows directionality and he already knows how to print his name. I decide to take a few minutes and see if he can use any letters of the alphabet to print the word ''pizza.'' I begin by saying, ''George, that was great the way you wrote down my order. You could also have written the word pizza another way using the sounds you hear in the word. Let me help you. You write and I'll help sound. Listen carefully. What sounds do you hear in P-I-ZZ-A? After much thought George replies, ''Z.'' ''Fabulous! How do you write that sound?'' ''Don't know!'' ''Well, let's look on the alphabet chart,'' and I point to the picture of a zipper and say, ''This letter Z makes that sound.'' George carefully copies it. ''Bravo George.'' As I leave, George is proudly showing his fellow waiters two ways to write pizza. I quickly make a note to myself on George's writing folder.

Sept. 5. Playing in pizza parlor used writing to take order and read it back accurately. Worked on hearing sounds in word ''pizza.'' Wrote Z. Continue to have him hear and record letters of the alphabet in his writing.

Scene 3. Susan

I asked Susan, a self-composed six-year-old, to bring me a story that she would like to share. She brought *How Do I Put It On?* by Shigeo Watanabe, and settled herself to read. Susan imitated the stance and movements that I use when I read a story. She crossed her legs, swiveled her chair, and tilted the book toward me so I could see the pictures and proceeded to read the title and point out the author's name saying, "This is the person who wrote this book." Then she carefully opened the book and page by page "read" the pictures. "Once upon a time there was a little bear who always put his clothes on wrong. First he tried to put his hat on his feet." The story was right but the words were not those printed on the page.

Susan knows a lot about books and stories. She knows how to recognize the title and find the author's name, how to hold a book, where to begin a story, how to turn the pages and, most importantly, that the pictures help to tell the author's story.

When Susan has finished reading her version, I praise her for reading the pictures so well. Then I say, "Let's have a look at what the words say." I drag my finger under the words, moving smoothly across the page as I read the text. Susan watches and joins in with "No, I put it on like this!" At the end of the conference I help Susan to fill in her reading log and make a note to myself.

Oct. 7. How Do I Put It On? — enjoyed the story but so far not paying attention to words. Worked on being aware of print on the page. Must re-read with her soon then send book home. NB Does she read at After-School Care?

Scene 4. Pedro

Pedro, a recently arrived member of our class from San Salvador, shyly approaches me with the picture dictionary. Pedro is eight, speaks fluent Spanish, and can read and write simple stories in Spanish. According to his Heritage Language Instructor and his parents he loves stories and is keen to pursue his interest in reading and writing. His parents want to borrow stories in Spanish from our classroom and school libraries to read with him at home.

In the classroom Pedro loves class story time and I have observed him picking up the book I have just read and looking intently at the pictures. He often asks me, "What does this say?" Because Pedro is already literate in his first language, I know he is at an advantage in learning his second language, English. The stronger the learner's literacy skills are in his first language, the easier it is for him or her to transfer these skills to another language. I decide to try to use Pedro's already well-developed

Spanish skills to help him learn English.

We begin to look at the pictures in the dictionary. Pedro points to a picture and says the word in Spanish. I say it in English. "El automovil," "Car"; "La Casa," "House"; "El perro," "Dog." Sometimes I ask Pedro a question such as, "Do you have a dog?" "Do you like bananas?" Many times he answers, showing me that he understands more than he can speak.

At the end of this brief conference I ask Sam to go with Pedro to ask his Heritage Language teacher for a Spanish-English picture dictionary. I make a note in his reading log.

Sept. 15. At next session start a bilingual dictionary with Pedro choosing own words and pictures. Make sure he is included in as many small-group activities as possible — include him in cooking with Mrs. G.

I also decide to see if there is an older student in the school who is bilingual in Spanish and English who would benefit from reading with Pedro on a regular basis. If I can organize three 15-minute sessions per week with stories in both English and Spanish I am confident that Pedro, with his keen desire to learn, will begin to make good progress in English. Fortunately, Vincente, a grade six boy, is willing to help and for whom extra reading aloud is of great benefit. Soon his teacher and I have set up a buddy program and both boys begin to make progress in their reading skills.

Scene 5. Justin

I am sitting at the writing table with six children who are composing their stories. Justin, sitting on my right, is five years old at the start of his senior kindergarten year. He has drawn his picture and now wants to write a sentence describing what is happening in the picture. He waits; I have to encourage him to start. Justin would like me to write the sentence for him so that he could copy it. I know that if I do this, however, he will not learn how to find the sounds he needs to make the words he wants to say. We begin by talking about the picture. He is making a book about insects; his picture shows an insect hovering above some flowers under the stars. "Tell me about your picture," I ask. "The moth flies from flower to flower," he replies. "Is that what you want to write? OK. That's your first sentence. Which word comes first?" We say the sentence again and Justin tells me that "the" is the first word. "OK. So how do you write 'the'?'' He looks at me hopefully. The word is so commonly used that I often say T-H-E — the letter names — and this triggers the children's memory. Justin writes, saying T-H-E to himself as he writes the letters before waiting patiently for more help. I am working with the child on my left while he writes. When I turn back to him he has forgotten what word comes next, so we recap. I place one unifix brick for each of the words on the table, marking each spoken word with a brick. "The-moth-flies-from-flower-to-flower." Seven bricks. "You've written the first one, now what's next?" "Moth," says Justin. "What sounds do you hear in moth?" "Mmm," says Justin. This is one he knows and he writes M. Then I help him with **oth**, sounding out the short vowel and blending it with the **th** sound. "Look, here's TH saying **th** again just like in the." Justin spells "moth" and then reads his words again "The moth-flies. I know. That starts with F," he says. "Great! You are really doing well." When I next turn to Justin he has written, "The moth FLS FM," and he is starting to write "flower." I continue to help him find the sounds he wants, using the alphabet strip pasted on the table in front of us to help him locate the letter W to make the **wer** sound in flower. Justin is content with FLS for flies, FM for from, and FW for flower. I do not try to make him spell these correctly. The main help that he needs right now is the confidence to represent words with letters fast enough to be able to hold meanings in his head. If he spends too long on spelling, he forgets what he wants to say. "Look how much you've written already! You're doing a great job. Keep going."

While I work with other children, Justin continues to write. He finishes the sentence "the moth flies from flower to flower" and decides to add "eating flies. They come out at night." This is written relatively quickly with help only for the **ing** of eating. Justin represents those words with tu CM Aot At nAtw.

the moth FLS Fm FW toF
etinp FS. tU CM Aot At nAtw

The finished piece shows me a great deal about Justin's current knowledge of spelling and writing: he spells phonetically; he has represented each syllable with a letter; he is fairly confident with the sounds made by the consonants, but not yet sure about the vowels, in fact, he doesn't always use a vowel; and he is aware of upper- and lower-case letters and uses them randomly. From spending time with Justin as he composed the piece, I know that he is unsure of his ability to spell and needs reassurance that it is okay to put what he thinks; that once he begins to write it is easier for him to trust his own judgment; and that he is fairly articulate and understands that print is anything you say written down. With daily writing time and lots of reading Justin is well on the way to "cracking the code." In my record book I jot down:

Oct. 10. Phonetic spelling; becoming aware of vowels; needs confidence to sound out for himself.

Scene 6. Randy

Randy has come to me for his book-sharing time. He brings *The Very Quiet Cricket* which we have read as a class and which has captured the children's attention because of the cricket's chirp that is found at the back of the book. "Oh good, I love this one. Can you tell me the title?" "The Very Quiet Cricket," says Randy. "Where does it say that?" He points to the words on the cover. "And what about these words?" I say, pointing to the author's name. "Don't know," he replies so I tell him that this is the name of Eric Carle who wrote the book and made the pictures. We open the book at the first page. "Where does the writing start, Randy?" He points to the beginning of the first line. "That's right." I begin to read and use my finger to point to each word as I say it. I know that this text is too difficult for Randy to read, but there are parts where he will be able to join in. The text is repetitive in that every insect that the little cricket meets speaks to him, but the little cricket cannot reply because he hasn't yet learned to chirp. Each page ends with the words "Nothing happened. Not a sound." The book offers us a great opportunity to read together. When I get to the pattern, I stop and wait for Randy to join in. By half way through I am able to stop reading and let Randy read the pattern. We don't have time to finish the book together, but he takes it away to read on his own and I promise him that we can finish next time. In my record book I note:

Nov. 7. Randy very enthusiastic to read. Using pictures to predict words. Chiming in. No one-to-one correspondence of word to print yet.

Scene 7. Alison

Alison is reading *I Like Books* by Anthony Browne, which she knows by heart. As she turns each page she reads the picture first to remind herself of the words. A picture of a monkey about to step on a banana peel reminds her that the words are "Funny book"; the same monkey singing cues, "Song books." When we get to "and strange books," however, she sees a picture of a fish swimming out of the cover of a book and reads "and books about fish." "Let's take another look at that one, Alison. Point to the first word and say it." "And." "Yes, now what about the second word? You said books, can it be books?" "No it's got an S." "That's right. Any ideas?" Alison has forgotten so I read "strange," not wanting to labor the point. She says, "It really is strange a fish coming out of a book!" I note:

March 6. Confident with known text with pattern and rhyme. Starting to see initial letters as a clue to unlocking a word. Needs to focus on this. Suggest moving her to First Steps books without patterns.

Scene 8. Ranjit

Ranjit brings *I Like Books* by Anthony Browne, which he has not read. "What do you think it's about?" I ask. "Reading," he replies. "Yes, it's about lots of different books. Let's read it together. "I like books." On every page the word "book" appears. As we come to the word, I ask Ranjit to join in with me and we point to it. By the end of the book, he recognizes the word and says it without my prompt. He says books about monsters are his favorite.

Sept. 30. Enjoys books. Sees print going from left to right. Knows what is a word and a letter. Chimes in. No one-to-one correspondence yet. Recognizes words when they repeat. Could find word "book" on every page. Needs lots of experience with pattern books. Use rhymes with him?

Scene 9. Chen

Chen is a perplexing child. He is a lively six-year-old who has been in our school since junior kindergarten. Although he can make his basic needs known, his command of English remains limited. His Heritage Language instructor reports that his command of Chinese is also minimal. At home he speaks in one-word and short sentences about everyday occurrences. Chen can print his name but when asked to write, draw, or paint he produces work like this.

At story time Chen is easily distracted, preferring to play with the blocks or bin toys, which he looks at longingly. During the work period he never chooses the book corner as an activity. As well, he does not volunteer to take books home for his family to share with him and has to be constantly reminded to take his bookbag from school to home and back again.

In searching for something that will help Chen to become hooked on books I enlist the help of an older Chinese-speaking student, Mei Ling, who comes every day to read with Chen for 10 minutes. It is Mei Ling who makes the breakthrough! She discovers that Chen loves the *Spot* books where you lift the flap to find the puppy hidden beneath. I quickly collect a selection of lift-the-flap books and we begin to work with these in both English and Chinese. I read them in English and Mei Ling and Chen's Heritage Language instructor read them in Chinese. We put these books into his bookbag for his family to read at home. When Chen can read a book by memorization, he goes to the Parenting Center in the school to read with the toddlers. Slowly, we begin to see him start to take an interest in books.

I ask Chen to represent his thinking in pictorial form every day. It might be a painting, a drawing, or a map of his building, but he must represent and he must speak with me about it. "Tell me about your drawing, Chen." I use repetition and gentle prompts such as "Tell me a bit more" or "Say something more about that" to encourage him to elaborate his answers and clarify what he means. It is a breakthrough when Chen produces the following piece of work, complete with speech bubbles and written labels.

Conferencing with the Developing Reader and Writer

Scene 1. Nicole

Nicole, a seven-year-old, has just made the transition from a beginning reader to a developing reader. She can now read simple picture books that have no pattern or rhyme. When writing, she uses several accurate letters for each word and is beginning to space and use correct spelling constructions for words such as the, and, is, and girl.

At our bi-weekly individual reading conference, she brings *On Mother's Lap* by Ann Herbert Scott to share. I know from her reading log that she has not read this book before so I make a point of helping her to access prior knowledge that might help her with the reading. We examine the cover, speculating what the book will be about, and what the mother and the little boy might do. I ask, "Who will sit on mother's lap?" because I want to give her the word "lap," reasoning that it might be a difficult word for her to unlock successfully from the picture. Together we look through the illustrations, talking about what is happening. For pages that have difficult or unusual vocabulary, I provide cues through my questions, giving her the name of the boy and the word "reindeer." "Do you think Michael will have room for his reindeer blanket on his mother's lap? You do? Let's turn the page and see if you're right. You are! There's his reindeer blanket tucked around Boat and Dolly." When we have looked through the book, I ask Nicole to read the story to me. With some assistance she reads the story word for word, carefully pondering what the text might say. At the end I ask her to tell me what she thought the story was about and she replies, "It's about a boy who's jealous of his baby sister!" I know then that she has understood what she has read. Nicole's reading of this story has been a search for meaning.

At the end of this 15-minute session, I ask her to fill in her reading log with the title of the book, the date read, who was involved in the reading, and a personal comment about the experience. I also make a note:

Jan. 15. Well done Nicole! You must share this book with your buddy-reader and your Mom and Dad. They will be proud of you!

I finish the conference by asking her to select another book from the same bucket to read next time we met. She selects *Gone Fishing* by Earlene Lung.

Scene 2. Sam

Sam greets me with the words, "I want to do a project about sharks! My brother's doing one on frogs but mine's going to be about sharks. I know a lot about sharks. We saw some when we went to the aquarium." I reply, "Super! How will you begin?" "I don't know. Maybe I'll draw some pictures and write some stuff." "That sounds like a good plan to me. Why don't you go away and make a list of all the facts you know about sharks. Number each fact starting at 1. Here, let me help you begin." I take a large sheet of paper and print #1 at the top. Sam prints this:

#1 SRS et fes

Sharks eat fish.

I print #2; Sam goes away to complete his list of information about sharks. The next day he shows me his completed work.

1. Sharks eat fish.
2. Sharks live in the water.
3. The shark is looking at the fish because they look delicious.
4. Sharks are big and little.

From his writing I know that Sam knows a lot about print. He uses most of the letter sounds correctly, uses spaces, and uses the same letter combinations for a word each time he spells it, for example, he spells "thay" the same way each time. Initially, I decide not to focus on the surface features of Sam's work but to help him expand his ideas. Together, we read his work and put a check mark beside all the facts of which he is absolutely sure.

Sam goes to the library to get a book to check the facts about which he is not positive. With the teacher-librarian's help he makes the following changes.

The next day Sam and I meet briefly. I ask him to write two questions he would like answered about sharks. Here are his questions.

That night I send the questions and a book on sharks home with him, including a note to his parents asking them to help Sam find the answers.

#1 HO R BABS BN

How are babies born?

#2 O RTHR WNMS

Who are their enemies?

Dear Mr & Mrs Katsuras,
   Please help Sam find the answers to
these two questions. I have included some
books to help you.
                    Yours
                      h. Hart.

Three days later Sam proudly comes to school with the following information.

#1 ALV FRM the MMS

STMC

#2 PEPL that et SHaRK

1. Alive — from the moms stomach.
2. People — they eat shark.

We are now almost ready to publish this work. Sam decides he wants to make a diorama of sharks in the ocean. He will put all the information he has found on cards and attach them to the diorama. Several days later Sam's diorama is finished and it is time to add the written work. Together we make headings and group the information accordingly. We find the fastest way is to cut and paste.

Where they live

SRS LV (shark) NstWotR

tha iz wem wotr

Food

SRS et fes

Sharks

Babies Sharks are born

ALV FRM tHeMrs STMC

Enemies

+2. PCPL tha et SHaRK they shark

they

At this point, I help Sam with the editing process, showing him the correct spelling for "they" and "shark." He carefully corrects these words and adds them to the list of 4-5 words at the front of his writing folder. Sam knows that before he brings any work to me for sharing he must check to make sure the words on the list are spelled correctly. When I see Sam has mastered a word he crosses it off, using a highlighter.

Sam leaves his corrected work for our parent volunteers to type. The next day, I give him a clean copy of his work to cut and paste to his shark diorama. Sam's shark project takes three weeks from start to finish. At the end he proudly agrees to have his work on display in the library for others in the school to enjoy.

Scene 3. Georgina

Georgina hurries up to me with a book about puppies in her hand saying, ''I need to know how long before puppies can eat food. My dog had four babies.'' Georgina loves to look at books and is often to be found snuggled up in the book corner reading to her favorite doll or stuffed animal. From her reading log I realize that Georgina has never read a piece of non-fiction for herself. Up to now her choices have ranged from fairy tales to stories about families to lift-the-flap books. This seems like a good opportunity to teach Georgina some of the features of non-fiction materials.

The book she has found is particularly good for this short lesson. It has excellent pictures, just a few lines of text on each page and, unlike the narrative work Georgina is familiar with, has bold headings that group the information. We start by looking at the cover. I explain that books like this one are different from stories because of the headings. On each page of the book is a picture and a large heading that tells the reader what the page is about. We read Just Born, Feeding Time, and Exploring in Angela Rayston's *See How They Grow: Puppy*. After briefly examining the 32-page book, I ask Georgina to find the pages that would tell us when puppies are ready to eat real food. After a few minutes, during which time I deal with several other children's requests, Georgina finds the appropriate page. When I ask her to read it with me, she has little difficulty with the words and is able to draw on her extensive knowledge about dogs and puppies to help her unlock words such as ''milk.''

When she has finished, I make a note in her reading log.

Nov. 16. Ask Georgina to read other non-fiction materials.

In my record book I note:

Do a shared writing lesson with Georgina and several other students who could benefit from looking closely at non-fiction materials through use of big books. Perhaps a small interest center on pets if other children are interested?

Scene 4. Agip

Agip is a quiet seven-year-old who attacks every activity he selects or is assigned with precision and intense concentration. When I ask him what book he wants to share with me he holds up *Mine's the Best* by Crosby Bonsall. We look at the front cover and talk about what the story might be about. He thinks it is about animals and what lives in water. I am uneasy with his answer, but I decide to press on with the reading and listen carefully while Agip reads the story. He reads accurately, word by word, even offering some expression, however, when I ask him at the end to tell me about the story he answers, "I can't." "What was the story about Agip?" "I don't know." "Was it about animals?" I ask. "Sort of." Clearly, Agip has said the words but not understood them. Reading this story has not triggered understanding and meaning. "Let's go back and have another look at it." We turn the pages and I discuss with Agip what is happening on each page as two children argue about who has the best water toy. As we talk, I realize that Agip has no experience of water toys and consequently has no background knowledge to help him make sense of the words. I make a note of our conference in his reading log.

Dec. 7. Agip read fluently but couldn't retell the story. Lacked understanding of what he had read. Must check his writing folder to see the scope of his writing. What else can I do to help his comprehension?

The follow-up: Looking at his reading and writing for the last six weeks I realized that Agip knew a lot about print and stories. His writing made sense to him and he could talk about it. Topics, however, were confined to his family, T.V., and his visit to his cousins.

I decided to use these topics as springboards for future reading and collected simple books about families and trips to the store to share with Agip. I checked throughout the course of his reading that he was making sense of what he read. Parent volunteers were made aware that some children can read without understanding so that they, too, would ask questions that checked understanding as they listened to children read. I also included Agip in several group activities — planting, simple experiments, cooking — in which information was recorded that helped the group perform the task. For a while Agip was bombarded with the question, "What does this sentence tell us to do?" Slowly, my notes showed that over time, he began to make more sense of what he was reading, but still required a lot of adult assistance to reflect and question what the words mean.

Scene 5. Aileen

Aileen is reading *Peter's Chair* by Ezra Jack Keats. She comes to the word "remember" and stops. When she looks at me, I suggest she read ahead. "Go on, miss it out and come back." She reads, "We have a new baby in the house." "Now, look at this word again. What do you think his mother is saying to him?" Aileen is stuck on remember and guessing from the context is not going to help. "What else could you try?" "I could sound it out." "OK, let's divide up the word into its parts." I place my finger over the word so that only **re** is showing. Aileen is able to read it. Then I show her **mem**, which she reads correctly. When she looks at **ber**, Aileen recalls that we talked about words that ended in **er** in a mini-lesson. She realizes that the word is remember and reads the whole sentence again. I make a note in my record book.

Jan. 17. Worked on syllables; showed Aileen how to look for clues within the word.

Conferencing with the Fluent Reader and Writer in the Early Years

Scene 1. David

I have been watching David, who is eight years old, for several days during writing workshop. He concentrates on his work, persevering throughout our writing time and carefully storing the pages in his folder to be retrieved next day. He is writing his own version of the story *Paddle-to-the-Sea* by Holling Clancy, which I read in installments to the class. At last it is done and he wants to read it to me.

There are six pages of closely written text. This is the first page. I notice that David has listed some things that he intends to include in his story and a key to remind himself that these are important. It's a sort of table of contents!

Paddle-to-the-Sea!

THINGS

Paddle
Cabbin
Pond | River
Bever dam
Bever

IMPORTINT

① Once in a Plase called Nippigon there was a Boy and He Made a boat and he Put It on a Snow bank and he Was hoping that It wold slide Down into the Pond and it did some and the wood cutters left Some wood by a Streem and thay ware Wating untell Spring So the wood wold Go down the streem

David reads out loud and I listen. I find it easier at this stage if I don't look at what the children have written. Instead, I watch their faces and listen intently, making sure that I understand what they mean. It helps me to concentrate on the meaning and it also shows them that I am interested in their ideas, not in the look of the piece. David reads his writing fluently and with expression. There is considerable pride in his voice as he nears the end of the story. Now we have some decisions to make. Does he want to publish this piece or go on to something new? David decides that he wants to start a new story. He doesn't want to edit and revise his Paddle-to-the-Sea story. He's tired of it and wants to do something different. I agree to this plan. The writing is a considerable achievement and quite a bit longer than anything he has written before. Before I let him put the story away, however, I look to see if there are points that David can learn from. Can we set some goals for his next piece of writing? What is he doing well that I can build on?

The story certainly flows. Based on a well-loved tale it is a retelling and as such has few problems with structure. Much of the language, however, is David's. I compliment him on his choice of words and the way he has made the story come alive. I love the way he says ''he was hoping it would slide down into the pond and it did!'' using larger letters and underlining for emphasis. I notice that he has substituted ''some'' for ''the'' and I tell him that I am pleased to see him choosing his words carefully. I am trying to convince the class that crossing out a word because you have thought of a better one is a sign of a thoughtful writer.

There are some points about spelling that we could discuss — place, stream, they, were, would — and I ask him to check his word book to see if he has the correct spelling of these words recorded and to use an eraser to change the places in his draft where these are misspelled. In addition, I decide that David needs a mini-lesson on sentences. He is writing oral language, without punctuation; he is ready to learn about the use of the period to signal the end of each complete thought. David could also vary his sentence structures when indicating the passing of time — ''and then'' seems to predominate throughout the piece as a linking device. He needs to choose words and phrases like next, soon after, much later, and the next day to bring variety and more precision to the temporal sequence of his story. We talk about these words and I write them at the back of his folder in the section ''Things I'm Learning About Writing.''

David asks if he can read his story to the class. At sharing time he takes the author's chair and everyone enjoys the story. As he reads I notice that he is able to pause as if his work were written in complete sentences. He has internalized the concept of a sentence, so is ready to learn how to mark it in punctuation. I make a note to myself.

Feb. 18. Hold a mini-lesson on sentences with David and one or two others who are ready to apply this skill to their writing.

Scene 2. Kimmy

Kimmy, who is also eight, loves the "Care Bears" and has written a story called "The Care Bears Help Out." It has a beginning, a middle, and an end. There is a problem — a boy and a girl who quarrel are taken by "No-Heart" to his castle. The Care Bears rescue them and everyone plays together happily.

up up up in the Clowds
the caRe BeaRs weRe
Playing happiLie. SLiding
down Rainbows then they
Lookd undeR the clowds and
saw a giRL and a boy fiting.
STop That you make
frieds said Wish Bear
I WILL Play with You But
they said No so wish Bear
told the otheR BeaRs This is.
A Jobe foR the caRe Bears

When Kimmy reads the story to me she clearly knows where the sentence breaks occur. She uses expression, especially when her characters speak. Her writing, however, shows me that she hasn't understood how to place a period at the end of a sentence. Here's another candidate for a mini-lesson on sentences.

We could also talk about using quotation marks around direct speech, but I think this may be best left until her writing shows that she has understood sentences.

Kimmy wants to publish this piece so I circle some words for her to look up in the dictionary and the word bank. In her spelling notebook I make a list of words that sound like **ow** but are spelled **ou** — cloud, loud, proud, mouse, house, out — and I ask her if she can add one or two more when she comes across them in her reading. She goes away to edit her spelling and think about what form her published story will take.

In my record book I make a note about Kimmy's writing.

May 7. Another Care Bears story! She's showing growth in handling spelling (worked on ow/ou) and is ready to learn about punctuation — mini-lesson on periods for her as soon as possible. Can I suggest another topic to Kimmy? She's in a bit of a writing rut, only choosing to write about favorite cartoons or toys. I think it's time she worked on a piece of research — perhaps she'd be interested in writing about some of the animals mentioned in Paddle-to-the-Sea.

Scene 3. Brajit

Brajit is also eight and has recently become a fluent reader. She seemed to leap almost overnight from reading word by word to seeing the way that language flows and words work together. She has started to use all the cues simultaneously and so has moved from texts that support her through rhyme and rhythm and repetition to longer, more difficult reading. She has chosen Roald Dahl's *The Fantastic Mr. Fox* and I want to be sure that she is able to read it before she spends too much time on it. I'm not sure she has the stamina for a book this long. She reads the first page without hesitation but a little too hastily, and makes several miscues that don't make sense in her haste to show me how well she can read. I decide that I would like Brajit to write about this book as she goes along so that I can monitor her reading. I ask her to get her reading log and write a new heading, "The Fantastic Mr. Fox." I tell Brajit that I want her to stop at the end of each chapter and write a few sentences. At the back of her journal is a list of questions that we generated as a class, which are things to think about when reading. We go over these questions together.

Are you enjoying it? Why?
Is it exciting? Why?
What do you think is going to happen next?
Would you like to be there in this story?
What would you do if you were there?
Who do you like/dislike in the story? Why?

I tell Brajit that she is to choose one of these to write about each time and that I will reply to her writing. This journal will show me how well she is understanding the story. I make a note in my record book.

Mar. 1. Watch to see how much time she is taking to read each chapter — if she is struggling I'll suggest that she take it home and let her mother read the rest aloud to her.

Scene 4. Sara

Sara has read *The True Story of the Three Little Pigs* by Jon Scieska and Lane Smith that retells the story from the wolf's perspective. "Did you like it?" I ask. "Yes, it's funny. The wolf wasn't really bad, he just sneezed." "What happened when he sneezed?" "Well, he sneezed so hard he blew down the house and the little pig was in there and then he ate him." "What happened in the end?" "They put him in jail." "Why do you think they did that?" "Well, he was trying to break down the door of the third pig's house." "So what do you think — is it the true story? What really happened? Was he a Big Bad Wolf?" "I don't know. I don't think so." "Who is telling the story?" "The wolf." "Do you think perhaps a story changes when different people tell it from their point of view?" "Maybe." We read the last page of the book again and discuss what it means to "be framed." We talk about how the wolf sees the pigs as a legitimate source of food. I am not convinced that Sara has really understood the humor in the story, but she has certainly enjoyed it and found the pictures amusing. Working on telling a story from the point of view of one of the characters is something that we can do in a drama lesson. In pairs the children can interview each other. "Tell me what happened Granny, the day the wolf knocked on your door?"

May 5. Make a note to myself to include some story retelling from various perspectives the next time we work with a story in drama.

CHAPTER FIVE

Activities to Develop Reading and Writing Skills

Many of the word games and activities described in this section use common materials such as magazines, counters, paper, and pens. Where possible, suggestions are given for the words and phrases that make up the challenge of the activities.

As a further aid, the appendix includes a series of masters illustrating initial consonants, long and short vowels, consonant digraphs, and **y** words, which can be used with any number of the activities detailed in this section or as a supplement to those already in your classroom. Images have been chosen to reflect accurately the sounds we need to teach, for example, **b** is represented by bear; **c** by cat; and **d** by dog. An ideal situation is to involve children in illustrating their words (a word of warning — their drawings cannot always be recognized by others).

The Beginning Reader and Writer

Here are some activity suggestions that children can play together or with an adult. If parents can volunteer time in the classroom, these games are a great way to use their talents. Essentially, the games give practice and reinforce concepts that are being learned through the children's daily reading and writing. They are fun; they keep children occupied while you conference with others; and some can be made (in part) by the children, thus giving a sense of ownership. Make a special bag for children to use when they borrow the games to take home.

Game: Initial Consonant Bingo

Materials

- Initial Consonants Masters
- boards with eight squares
- pack of alphabet cards (initial consonants only)
- 32 blank cards
- pen
- old magazines
- scissors
- paste

Notes

Each child needs a board that shows eight pictures of everyday objects that begin with a variety of consonants. Some boards must contain the same words. Boards can be prepared in several ways: the children can draw pictures or cut them out of magazines and paste them on the boards, or you can photocopy the Initial Consonants Masters, and cut and paste the pictures on the boards. Write the name of the object under each picture.

This game can be expanded to include both consonants and vowels.

Instructions

1. Each player takes a board.
2. The pack of alphabet cards is placed face down on the table.
3. Each player takes a turn taking an alphabet card.
4. She or he shows the other players the card.
5. If any player has a picture that begins with that letter, she or he covers the picture on their board with a blank card.
6. The first person to cover all of his or her pictures wins.

Game: Track Games I

Materials

- Track Board Master
- dice or spinner
- markers
- Initial Consonants Masters (optional)

Notes

Track games can be adapted to help children learn a variety of skills. We suggest making generic track boards that can be used by changing the components of the games. Make a track with squares or shapes on it and a start and a finish line. At strategic points along the route, place hazard squares and bonus squares, for example, Go forward 2 spaces; Go back 3 spaces. The reading component comes in using Chance Cards. If a player lands on a Chance square she or he takes a card from the pile and reads it. Suggestions for Chance Cards include:

• alphabet letters — the child must say a word that starts with that letter before going on;
• words all beginning with the same initial consonant — the child reads the word and returns it to the pile. If they can't read it, they miss a turn;
• words beginning with a variety of initial consonants;
• words used on the class alphabet;
• instructions to find or to point to something, for example, find something beginning with **P**.

Instructions

1. Place the board in the center of the table.
2. Each player selects a marker.
3. All players place their marker at start.
4. Players take turns rolling the dice and moving their marker that number of spaces.
5. The first player to reach the end wins.

Activity: Collections

Start collections of objects that you can use to represent the letters of the alphabet. Children can help you by bringing discarded objects from home. Garage sales are a great source of interesting things for little cost! An old suitcase can be filled with things that all start with the same letter (a toy cat, a car, a doll's coat, a card, a candy). If possible, find tiny things that can be placed in a shoebox. Children love to play with these collections, sorting them, lining them up, and making up stories and games. Mix two collections and ask the children to sort them. A set of labels can be included and the children can match the words to the objects. They can play *I-spy* and *Grandmother Went to Market* using objects only.

Game: Beat the Board I

Materials

- boards with 12 squares
- series of word and letter cards
- pen
- old magazines
- paste
- scissors

Notes

The aim of the game, which is a form of solitaire, is to sort cards on a board, but the element of chance can always intervene to beat the player. If this happens and you are beaten by the board, you start again and play until you win! This game is exciting — the children read the words and letters in the game repeatedly as they try to beat the board. Like bingo and track games, Beat the Board can be adapted for any sound or set of words you want the children to practice. Here's how it works. Make a board with twelve squares. In 11 squares, draw pictures to illustrate the words you want the children to read or have the children draw or cut pictures. Label the remaining square in each board "OOPS." We suggest making several of these boards, using a variety of initial consonants on each board. Make a set of word/letter cards with the words on one side and the letters on the other. These correspond to the pictures on the board.

Instructions

1. The player places the cards word-side down on the board. (Do not match pictures and words).
2. Cover the OOPS square with a word/letter card.
3. The player identifies the letter that the picture showing represents.
4. She or he finds that letter card, places it word-side up on the picture, and reads the word.

5. Another picture is revealed. The player must find the card to cover that picture.
6. If the card the player needs is concealing the OOPS square, the board wins.
7. The player removes the cards from the board. She or he shuffles them and starts again. The goal is to complete the sorting before the OOPS square is revealed.

Game: Hopscotch Sounds

Materials

For outdoor Hopscotch
• chalk
• token, such as a stone or small block
• alphabet cards

For indoor Hopscotch
• plastic shower curtain
• masking tape
• token, such as a stone or small block
• alphabet cards

Notes

Young children are very physical and this game involves the whole body. If you can go outdoors, chalk a playing area on the playground. If you want to play indoors, buy a plastic shower curtain and divide it into squares using masking tape. Place an alphabet card in each square.

Instructions

1. A player tosses the token into the first square.
2. She or he hops onto the square.
3. The player must say the sound of the letter and think of a word beginning with that sound.
4. She or he picks up the token and returns to the start line.
5. The player tosses the token into the second square.
6. She or he continues until the token does not land inside the lines.
7. The next player takes a turn. When landing on the first,

second, third square, and so on, the player must think of another word for that letter.
8. Play continues until one player reaches the final letter and says a word that starts with that letter.

(* On subsequent turns the game becomes increasingly difficult. There are lots of variations that you can make up to add to this game. Ask the children for ideas.)

Activity: Alphabet Wheels

Make two circles of cardboard, one larger than the other. Cut a window about one inch square in the smaller circle. Join the circles in the center using a paper fastener. On the larger circle, print an initial consonant. In the window, draw a picture that represents the initial consonant sound. Move the window and print another initial consonant and draw a corresponding picture. Continue until you have a letter and a picture for each initial consonant. Children practice saying the sound, using the picture as a clue. These can be useful in conferences to check if children recognize initial consonant sounds.

Activity: Cut-Up Sentences or Puzzle Poems

This activity helps children to learn that words are individual items in a sentence separated by spaces, and that they are ordered across the page from left to right. It also helps them to memorize words by sight and reinforces concepts about print. If you interact with the children while they are doing this activity, you will have an excellent opportunity to see how their understanding of how print works is developing.

Choose a short text, such as a poem or nursery rhyme, that is of interest to the children. Ask a child to dictate a sentence from the text; write out his or her words. This makes it special for that child. Make three copies of the text that can be enlarged on cardboard for use on the floor or written in legible printing on standard-size paper. The big versions are fun for two children to play together while the smaller versions can be packaged in a plastic bag and lent for use at home. The first copy will serve as a master text to which the words will be matched. (We suggest you laminate the cardboard to increase the life of the game and make it look more attractive.)

Take the second version of your text and cut it into sentence strips. Individual words will be cut from the third version. Keep these in bags or use clothes pins to clip them together. There are a number of progressively difficult things that children can do with these word sets. They can match sentence strips to the master text; match individual words to the master; organize the sentences in the correct order without the master text in front of them; and arrange the text using the cut-up words. It can be fun to choose rhymes that are linked to study themes or to the seasons. Make a copy of the rhyme for each child to paste into a scrapbook — this will become a book of poems that they know well and can "read" by memorization.

The Developing Reader and Writer

Games that Increase Word Power!

Games give practice in reading and can be played by pairs of children, or with older buddies and parent volunteers. They can be used at odd moments as time fillers, when other activities are done, and to keep children busy while you work with other readers and writers. Some children love these sorts of games, others are not so keen. Keep your approach to these games open. Nothing teaches children to read faster than actually reading, whether from a book, a chart, or in the context of a game.

Some games may be useful to play when a child needs specific help with a concept. Jeff could not remember how to blend consonants and, when reading, would stop at a word beginning with a blend. A few games of Jaws using the pack of cards with consonant blends helped Jeff get over his blending block.

Activity: Sight Vocabulary

Word games help to build up a bank of high-frequency words that can be recognized and read quickly (sight words). There are many function words (e.g., like, the, and) that are used repeatedly to glue sentences together. They are difficult to learn because they don't refer to anything — their meaning comes from the work they do within the sentence, which is joining clauses and creating cohesion. Function words are structural words; they mark the grammatical or syntactic relationships between components in a sentence and are often easy to read in sentences because they can be predicted from the context. Read in isolation is a different matter. They need to be learned in context with other words that are meaningful. Again, it is probably from using them in their own writing that children learn such words. We put a card with the 100 most highly used words at the writing center for easy reference. The children can devise stories, poems, chants, or instructions that include these words.

---

100 High-Frequency Words

a about after all an and are as at be been but by called can come could day did do down each find first for from get go had has have he her here him his how if in into is it its like look long made many may more my new no not now number of oil on one or other out part people said see she so some than that the their them then these this time there to two up use was water way we were what when which who will with words would write you your

---

Skilled readers know a great number of words by sight, which they do not sound or break out into parts. A sight vocabulary is built through:

- extensive reading of many kinds of texts in a rich and balanced reading program;
- children's writing where they use common words over and over again;
- seeing the same words in many contexts, both inside and outside the classroom, for example, notices, signs, instructions, captions.

Game: Track Games II

Materials

- Track Game Master
- dice or spinner
- word cards
- counters
- markers
- pen
- blank cards

Notes

Use the same board that you used for teaching the consonants. Introduce new packs of cards for your track games that use the phonic information you want the children to practice at this stage. When they land on Chance squares, they read the cards. Here are some ideas for variations. Ask the children for ideas for adapting track games — they'll have lots of them!

Consonant Blends: Make a pack of cards with questions that use lots of words with blends, which the children must answer. If the answer is YES, they collect a bonus point (pick up a counter). At the end of the game they see how many counters they have. An alternative is to move forward on YES answers and stay in the same place or miss a turn on NO answers. Let the children decide the rules! Here are some questions you can use:

Can you blow a bubble?   *Can twins count to twenty?*
Does brown bread break? *Can spoons spell?*
Can clowns clap?   *Do you stop at a red light?*
Can crabs cry?   *Can trains swing?*
Is drink dry?   *Do you swap hockey cards?*

Can a flower fly a
plane? Do you trick or treat at Hallowe'en?
Is grass green? Can apples play the bagpipes?

After a child reads a card, she or he returns it to the bottom of the pack. The cards will be read frequently, becoming easier to read each time they are found. This gives opportunity for repeated reading in a fun context. The children are motivated by the game and find the reading enjoyable.

Magic-e: Put one word on a card. Use these cards to give practice with words that follow the "magic-e" rule (the magic-e at the end of a word makes the vowel say it's name). The child reads the word and takes a counter for each word read correctly. An alternative is to use these words to make up YES/NO sentences and play as in the blends game. A third idea is to make up sentences that are good news/bad news. In the Chance pile, use good news sentences such as:
Dad bakes a cake. Go on 2 spaces.
You play hide and seek at the lake. Go on 3 spaces.
You and your friend have the same name. Go on 3 spaces.

For the hazard squares, use bad news sentences such as:
There is an earthquake. Go back 4 spaces.
You fall on the ice. Go back 2 spaces.
You wake up too early. Go back 1 space.

Have the children use these word cards to make up sentences. They can make versions of the game for each other. Give them blank cards and see what they come up with! Here are some words for the magic-e rule:
bake, cake, fake, lake, make, quake, rake, shake, stake, take, wake
male, pale, sale, tale, whale
came, dame, fame, game, lame, name, same, tame
date, fate, gate, hate, late, mate
dice, lice, mice, nice, rice
hide, ride, side, tide
file, mile, pile, tile, while
dine, fine, mine, pine, shine, vine, whine
coke, joke, poke, woke

Onsets and rimes: Make a pack of cards using the 37 rimes (see p. 49). Make another pack of onsets: consonants, consonant

103

digraphs, and consonant blends. Place the two piles of cards beside the board. When a player lands on a Chance square, she or he takes an onset and a rime and puts them together. If the two make a word, the child moves forward two spaces. If the two don't make a word, the child goes back two spaces. As an example, a child picks up **ain** and **r**; the child can move forward two spaces because he has made the word "rain." Another child picks up **ain** and **d**; she moves back two spaces because "dain" is not a word.

Instructions

1. Place the board in the center of the table.
2. Each player selects a marker.
3. All players place their marker at start.
4. Players take turns rolling the dice and making up words.
5. If they are successful they move their marker that number of spaces.
6. If they are unsuccessful, they stay where they are or move back the stated number of spaces.
7. The first player to reach the end wins.

Game: Beat the Board II

Materials

- boards with 12 squares
- word cards
- old magazines
- paste
- scissors
- blank cards
- pen

Notes

Make a board with 12 squares. In one of the squares print "OOPS." Make sets of cards to play the game with. You need two of each of 12 words to play. Place one set of the words face up on the board, then cover them with the other set face down.

This saves making many bases. The same base can be used for any combinations of words.

- Make a version that uses only words that have initial consonant blends.
- Make a set that uses magic-e words.
- Give the children a set of 12 words using the 37 rimes, for example, r-ain, p-ain, g-ain, m-ain, b-ack, j-ack, p-ack, qu-ack, b-all, f-all, h-all, m-all.
- Make packs of words that are key vocabulary from class projects.
- Invite children to make a version of Beat the Board using any words they like. They can cut pictures from magazines and make word cards to match.

Instructions

1. The player places one set of cards on the board, word-side up.
2. She or he covers these cards with the other set of cards, word-side down.
3. Cover the OOPS square with a word/letter card.
4. The player tries to make a word from the two cards.
5. When she or he has made a word, play continues.
6. If the player can't make a word the board has won.
7. She or he removes the cards from the board, shuffles them, and starts again.

Game: Jaws

Materials

- cardboard strip (at least 4 inches long)
- small pieces of cardboard
- paper
- felt pens
- question cards
- pen
- plastic bags

Notes

Jaws is a fast-paced version of a track game played between two people, which children find fun to play. Make a track by folding a strip of cardboard four inches long into zig-zags, .5 in. deep, which represent waves. Each player makes a cardboard figure; one is a swimmer, the other, a shark. Question cards can be designed to practice any of the sounds, blends, vowel patterns, and key vocabulary. Keep game variations in plastic bags. The game can be changed to suit any topic, for example, a bird and a worm and Tyrannosaurus Rex and Stegosaurus.

Instructions

1. Players place the figures at the back of the strip (in the water).
2. At each turn a player must read a question card.
3. A YES answer permits a move of one wave; a NO answer means the player must stay in the same place.
4. If the swimmer gets to shore (end of the cardboard waves) first, she or he wins. If Jaws gets there first, the swimmer is in trouble!

Game: Cut-Up Words

Materials

- cards labeled with onsets
- cards labeled with rimes
- plastic bags
- pen
- paper

Notes

Make packs of cards and keep them in plastic bags. In each pack mix up onsets and rimes.

Instructions

1. Each player takes a bag of onsets and rimes.
2. Set a time (e.g., 30 seconds, 2 minutes, 5 minutes).
3. Each player tries to make as many words as they can in this time.
4. Each word players make must be recorded on a list.

(* An alternative is to have races between teams of two players. Start a class list using a roll of paper from a cash register. Mark off in 10s and 100s. No word can be repeated.)

Game: Rescuing a Prince

Materials

- marker
- cardboard
- blank cards
- colored markers
- rescuer
- dice or spinner

Notes

Co-operative games are track games with a difference. Players work together to get the marker to the end of the track. As they play, they read instructions and make decisions. Here is a game in which players must work together to save a prince.

Instructions

1. Brainstorm 10 obstacles that might prevent a rescue (e.g., a river, a dragon, an evil knight).
2. Brainstorm 16 ways to overcome these obstacles (e.g., a boat, a sword).
3. Make a board with 50 squares showing the path from the start to the finish.

4. Record the obstacles on the game board to block the path.
5. Record the solutions to obstacles on cards.
6. Make the rescuer.

To play:
1. One player deals the cards out to each of the four players.
2. The first player rolls the dice and moves the rescuer the indicated number of spaces.
3. When an obstacle is reached, the players must put down a solution card.
4. All players must agree with this solution.
5. If the player does not have a suitable card, another player can offer a solution.
6. If no solution is found that is agreeable to all players, the game ends — the prince has not been saved.
7. If an agreeable solution is found, the next player continues the game until the prince is rescued.

Activity: Magnet Fishing

Paper clips on the ends of word cards and two fishing rods with magnets keep children busy fishing for words to make sentences. High-frequency function words can be written on cards and combined with content words from a current theme to be put into the "fishtank."

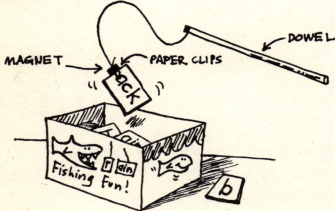

Activity: Sentence Rollers

You need three rollers, each with five sides made by folding cardboard into a solid pentagon. Write sentence starters on each face of the first roller, for example:

The little boy	*A white cat*	*A silly man*
A brave girl	*A mother hen*	*The big bad wolf*

Write sentence middles on each face of the second roller, for example:

went to the shops	*ran across a field*	*climbed a tree*
walked along the street	*jumped over a wall*	*swam across the pond*

Write sentence endings on each face of the third roller, for example:

to buy a loaf of bread	*and caught a cold*	*but couldn't get back again*
to see a movie	*and fell in a puddle*	*to find the pigs*

The children take turns to roll the three parts and see what sentences they can come up with. They can keep lists of their sentences or draw a picture of the one they like the best. They can also devise ideas for beginnings, middles, and endings to make their own set of rollers.

Activity: Crazy Characters Flip-Books

Another variation of the cut-up sentence idea involves making little books and marking the pages into three sections — top, middle, and bottom. The children decide on a character they would like to draw (e.g., people, animals, monsters, insects). On the top section of the page, the children draw the head and neck. On the middle section, they draw bodies that fit the necks. On the bottom, they draw legs that fit the bodies. Now come the captions. Name the character heads, for example, a baby, a policeman, a caterpillar. Put a verb phrase on the middle section, for example, was singing, went to the shops, was jumping, was eating a cabbage leaf. Write a prepositional phrase on the bottom section, for example, in the shower, on a bicycle, in a stroller, over the moon! Now cut the pages and turn the sections independently so you have the policeman's head, the caterpillar's body, the baby's legs, or other bizarre combinations. The sentence would read "A policeman was eating a cabbage leaf in a stroller." Great fun!

Activity: Phonics Wheels

Make two circles of cardboard, one larger than the other. Cut a window about one inch square in the smaller circle. Join the circles in the center using a paper fastener. On the large card, write a rime, for example, **ack**. In the window, write an onset, for example, **b**. Turn the top wheel round and write the rime and another onset in the blank window below it. Continue until you have as many words as you can fit on the wheel, for example, b-ack, h-ack, j-ack, l-ack, p-ack, qu-ack, r-ack, s-ack, t-ack, sh-ack, st-ack.

The children can play using a collection of these wheels. (They like to see how fast they can read them.) We have seen children in the house center trying to teach dolls to read using these wheels! They are useful during a reading conference to help teach a child to blend onsets and rimes.

110

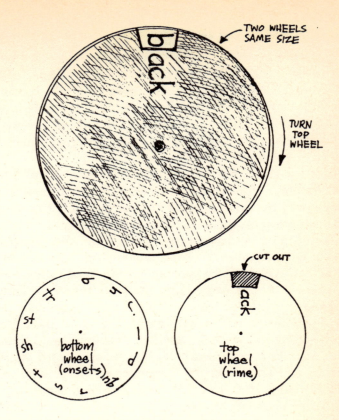

TWO WHEELS SAME SIZE

TURN TOP WHEEL

CUT OUT

bottom wheel (onsets)

top wheel (rime)

Activities: Word Banks and Dictionaries

Children at this stage are just beginning to edit their writing. They may look up the spelling of a word in a class dictionary or on a list kept in their writing folder. We choose one or two words in each piece of writing for children at this stage to correct. We may circle a word with a pencil and have the child come back when they have made the correction. We also keep a list of words on the front of the writing folder that they should check before showing their work to us.

Word banks can be ever-growing collections of words on cards, some illustrated, some not, arranged alphabetically, to which the children have easy access. They can be stored in file-card boxes, or in wall-pocket charts. We made one using 26 one-serving size cereal boxes and decorated them to be a train. It was attached to the wall at the children's eye-level. Children can add constantly to the collection of words and should develop the habit of using it to check their spelling.

The Fluent Reader and Writer

The activities for these children should make as much use as possible of their ability to use written language independently in real contexts. There are a myriad of ways in which communication skills can be developed through reading and responding to rich literature, writing and composing stories, poems, letters, and research reports, and viewing and representing ideas in a variety of media.

There are still times, however, when games and puzzles are useful to play. Word games draw attention to the sound of words and the way in which they are constructed. Collections of words focus attention on the structure and meaning of words. Games can focus on particular features of language, such as spelling patterns or word families. Words about feelings, words that describe characters, words that express movement or time or tension — these can be brainstormed and listed for reference during writing time.

Many games that play with words are listed and described by Larry Swartz in the book, *Spelling Links* by David Booth. Commercial games include Scrabble, Boggle, crossword puzzles, word searches, and Trivial Pursuit. Computer software is available to help children design their own activities such as crossword puzzles.

Any game idea can be taken and changed to fit a particular aspect of word-structure or meaning. Word searches can be designed, crossword puzzles created and solved, track games made and played, and games like Jaws adapted to fit interests and needs. Children can adapt and extend games for their own use. They can make games that challenge each other to define words, find definitions in the dictionary, and so on. Games that involve "beating your own record for speed" using digital watches or timers are popular. Involve the class in thinking about games, writing the rules, and organizing how they should be played. Most of all, have fun with words, explore them, enjoy them, and use them creatively.

In conclusion, once children are Fluent Readers and Writers they will make the most progress in developing their mastery of the spelling system by reading and writing. Games provide ways to practice and consolidate knowledge, but the classroom in our view, should be a place where language is used for learning and is learned in use.

Appendix

Track Games Master
Initial Consonants Masters
Consonant Digraphs Master
Long and Short Vowels Masters
Y Words

Track Games Master

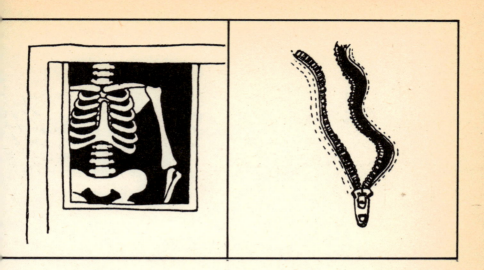

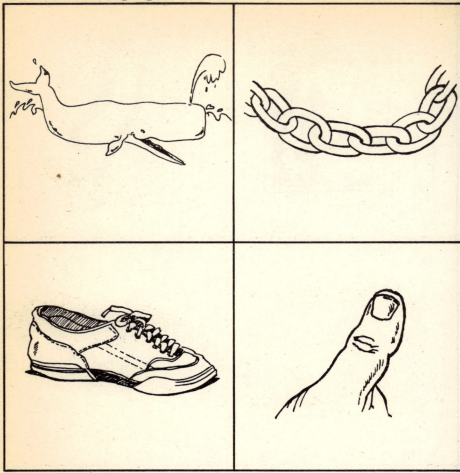

Long and Short Vowels

Bibliography

Professional References

Adams, Marilyn Jager. (1990). *Beginning to Read: Thinking and Learning About Print*. Urbana-Champaign, IL: Center for the Study of Reading, University of Illinois.

Booth, David. (Ed.). (1991). *Spelling Links*. Markham, ON: Pembroke Publishers.

Calkins, Lucy McCormick. (1986). *The Art of Teaching Writing*. Portsmouth, NH: Heinemann.

Cambourne, Brian. (1988). *The Whole Story*. Auckland, NZ: Ashton-Scholastic.

Hart-Hewins, Linda, & Wells, Jan. (1990). *Real Books for Reading: Learning to Read with Children's Literature*. Markham, ON: Pembroke Publishers.

Snow, C.E. (1990). "Rationales for Native Language Instruction: Evidence from Reserch." In A.M. Padilla, H.H. Fairchild, & C.M. Valadez, *Bilingual Education: Issues and Strategies*. Newbury Park, CA: Sage, pp. 60-74.

Children's Literature

Bonsall, Crosby. (1984). *Mine's the Best*. New York, NY: Harper & Row.

Browne, Anthony. (1988). *I Like Books*. London, UK: Julia McCrae Books.

Carle, Eric. (1990). *The Very Quiet Cricket*. New York, NY: Philomel Books.

Clancy, Holling. (1980). *Paddle-to-the-Sea*. Boston, MA: Houghton Mifflin.

Dahl, Roald. (1978). *The Fantastic Mr. Fox*. New York, NY: Bantam.

Hill, Eric. (1980). *Where's Spot?* New York, NY: Putnam.

Hoffman, Mary, & Binch, Caroline. (1991). *Amazing Grace*. New York, NY: Dial Books for Young Readers.

Hughes, Ted. (1968). *The Iron Man*. London, UK: Faber & Faber.

Keats, Ezra Jack. (1967). *Peter's Chair*. New York, NY: Harper & Row.

LeGuin, Ursula. (1988). *Catwings*. New York, NY: A Little Apple Paperback, Scholastic.

Lung, Earlene. (1984). *Gone Fishing*. Boston, MA: Houghton Mifflin.

McPhail, David. (1982). *Pig Pig Rides*. New York, NY: Dutton.

Rayston, Angela. (1991). *See How They Grow: Puppy*. Richmond Hill, ON: Scholastic Canada.

Scieska, Jon, & Smith, Lane. (1981). *The True Story of the Three Little Pigs*. New York, NY: Viking.

Scott, Ann Herbert. (1992). *On Mother's Lap*. Boston, MA: Clarion Books.

Watanbe, Shigeo. (1982). *How Do I Put It On?* London, UK: Penguin.

Index